Santa Shoes

A Mt. Hope Southern Adventure Book Five

Lynne Gentry

Travel Light Press

For information on how to join Lynne Gentry's Reader's Club visit www.lynnegentry.com

Cover photo by Shutterstock

Cover design by Lynne Gentry

Edited by Janet Johnson

Print ISBN: 9780998641270

Summary

A second chance is the greatest gift.

Christmas is only weeks away, but no one in Mt. Hope is feeling very festive. Main Street is on the verge of becoming a ghost town. Leona Harper Levy believes resurrecting the annual Christmas parade is the only way to give the dying small town a second chance.

But Leona's extravagant plan hits a snag when she realizes there's no one to play Santa . . . unless the scruffy drifter the wind blew in was sent by God.

Humor, heart, and hope come together in the Harper family's second-chance holiday story.

Join the thousands of fans who've laughed until they cried while rooting for Leona and all the quirky citizens of the small, dusty West Texas town of Mt. Hope.

www.lynnegentry.com

Also By Lynne Gentry

MT. HOPE SOUTHERN ADVENTURES

Walking Shoes

Shoes to Fill

Dancing Shoes

Baby Shoes

Santa Shoes

WOMEN OF FOSSIL RIDGE

Flying Fossils

Finally Free

First Frost

MEDICAL THRILLERS

Murder on Flight 91

Ghost Heart

Port of Origin

Lethal Outbreak

Death Triangle

SCI-FI/TIME TRAVEL/HISTORICAL

The Carthage Chronicles

For My Readers

Your enthusiasm for the fine folks of Mt. Hope

has cheered me on.

Chapter One

Leona

The old furnace in the chilly newspaper office coughed and sputtered. The unit wasn't the original steam boiler installed when the building was built in 1902, but the current gas furnace hadn't been replaced since Ivan Tucker's father bought the two-story brick building in1972.

Leona's breath puffed white as her blue fingers hovered above her computer keyboard. "Lord," she whispered. "Don't let the heat go out before we put the paper to bed."

As if the ancient fan motor had heard her prayers, the old machine wearily rattled to life. Powdery pulpwood remnants floated in the lukewarm air drifting down from the fifteen-foot-high ceiling vents. The *Mt. Hope Messenger's* monthly issue had not been printed in-house for nearly three years, but the tang of newsprint and ink refused to vacate. If only newspaper subscribers had been so loyal.

Leona briskly rubbed enough feeling into her stiff fingers to push *send* on the latest article she'd written. For weeks, she'd been working to convince the county commissioners to add more BRIDGES ICE IN WINTER signage along the narrow farm-to-market roads. At the last county commissioners' meeting, she'd even shared her son-in-law Parker's *Old Farmer's Almanac* prediction of an early winter. Today's unseasonable drop into the freezing-temperature range in early November proved two things: the almanac was never wrong, and Parker Kemp had been the perfect rehire for his old job at the County Extension office.

Ever since the perilous trip her family made to visit Parker and Maddie in the jungles of Central America, she'd been praying for their return to Mt. Hope . . . when they felt the time was right, of course. If she'd learned anything from dating her old missionary friend Roy McGee, it was that you could take the missionary out of the field, but you couldn't take the love of serving on the field out of the heart of someone truly called.

And so, when the Lord opened the perfect doors for her kids to come home sooner than she'd expected, she'd held her breath. Leaving the mission field was a big life change. And she knew as well as anyone the toll life changes could take on a person. But she would be the first to admit that she was glad when Parker and Maddie chose to bring her grandchildren back to the States.

If the Lord could answer such a tricky prayer with such perfection and speed, why was he dragging his feet on her request to add a few more warning signs to the county roads? Taking this hazardous situation public was a last resort, one she seldom resorted to, but winter was coming. And she could think of no other way to get the commissioners to do the right thing. Not that adding her two cents to the considerations would make a hill of beans to the few remaining commissioners trying to shore up the county's sinking budget. But she would sleep better knowing she'd done everything possible to avoid having to write any more articles about another pickup plunging into one of the county's many dry creek beds.

Leona closed her laptop and let her gaze drift to the dark clouds gathering outside the large office windows. According to the brittle newspapers stuffed in a box in the back room, Mt. Hope's Main Street had once bustled with cowboys and homesteaders. These rough and tumble men spent their paychecks at the town's five saloons. Fights and shootings were common Saturday night entertainment.

Law and order were established when churches like Mt. Hope Community church came in. The trouble soon died down, but so did the town.

In truth, she knew that adding ice warning signs were the least of this town's worries. It had been days since a single car had parked on either side of Main Street. Across the empty street, florescent lights lit the inside of Brewer's Auto & Tractor Parts. She hadn't seen a single shopper go in or out of Roxie's parts store all day. And the few remaining area ranchers or farmers who used to come to town to grab the blue-plate special at Ruthie's diner and buy their tractor parts at Brewer's, no longer had to shut down their agricultural operations when a piece of equipment broke down. They simply pulled out their phone, ordered a replacement part online, then went right back to farming or ranching until the part was delivered to their door.

Gone were the days when Mt. Hope bustled with business. Gone were the days when hope was something this small town believed in.

Sadness settled heavy on Leona's shoulders. What good would it do to add warning signs if there was no one left to read them?

Icy rain chipped away at the *Mt. Hope Messenger* words Ivan's father, Hiram Tucker, had painted on the newspaper office glass when he opened his press in this old building. If she didn't come to a decision soon, this window would be boarded over like most of the other businesses in this dying rural community.

She'd put off talking to Saul about Ivan's offer to sell her the newspaper. Which was crazy. Her second husband had always encouraged her to spend her first husband's money any way she saw fit. J.D. had left her so rich she didn't need anyone's approval. But in the three years she and Saul had been married, they'd become a team. She loved knowing she could depend on him for anything, including his undying support of her aspirations.

She would be the first to admit owning a newspaper was not the same as working for a newspaper. Managing everything from staff to subscriptions in a dying town would suck at more than her sizeable bank account. The effort would swallow the time she'd planned on investing in her family. With Maddie and Parker back from the mission field, and David and Amy up to their elbows in church work, her family needed her. J.D.'s death had taught her that time with family was something one should never take for granted. But something within her couldn't let go of the idea of owning her own newspaper and she knew exactly what that something was. Mt. Hope was home, and she was determined to do whatever she could to save it for those she loved.

Leona spun her desk chair. "Modyne, I just sent you an article to proof."

"Got it." The gray-haired woman who'd manned the newspaper office since the Tucker family opened shop, clicked away at her keyboard. Bleeding all over Leona's work was one of the old reporter's favorite past times.

"Thanks, Modyne," Leona searched her desk drawer for her gloves. "Send me the edits when you're done."

"Always do."

Instead of reminding Modyne that her job was to look for typos and not to interject her editorial opinions, Leona pulled on her gloves. "You're a peach, Modyne." And despite their differences, over the last few years she'd come to see how blessed she was to have learned so much from this woman.

"I'm a relic, and so are you." Modyne peered over her glasses. "Digital news is going to put us both out to pasture."

"Maybe, but I'm not going without a fight." Leona turned her attention toward Ivan.

The current owner and editor-in-chief of west Texas's only remaining small town newspaper stood at the coffee pot. He studied the rack of chipped coffee mugs as if he couldn't remember which cup he'd used for years. She'd been friends with Ivan Tucker and his wife Hathleen long before J.D. dropped dead at church. No one had been more surprised than she when the quiet church deacon hired her with only thirty years of church work experience on her resumé. Knowing she'd been a charity hire she did what any perfectionist would do, she'd set to work polishing her writing skills. Before long, Ivan expanded her writing assignments far beyond the obituaries. She and Ivan had had a compatible working relationship ever since.

Now, as she looked at her brave friend, her heart ached. Ivan had aged ten years in the year since Hathleen's death. His wife's unflappable support in the face of shrinking ad revenue had spurred Ivan to keep the newspaper afloat. Without Hathleen, Ivan had become lethargic and despondent.

Leona had first-hand experience with grief's ability to slump one's shoulders, so there was no judgment from her. In hopes of making life easier for Ivan, she'd happily taken on choosing the headlines, seeking more advertising dollars, and fielding the occasional complaint. But her efforts had proven as useless as a Band-Aid on an amputated arm. Ivan was hemorrhaging more than money. His passion for the newspaper business circled the drain.

Leona pushed her chair back from the desk. The rusty wheels squeaked across the scarred wooden floors. She stood and lifted her down-filled jacket off the seatback. "I think Romeo and I will head on to the hospital to work our therapy rotation before this weather gets any worse." At the sound of his name, her golden retriever and Great Pyrenes mix rose from his faithful place at her feet. The hundred-pound white-haired beauty stretched his big body. The swish of his fluffy tail sent pens and pencils flying from the top of Leona's desk.

"Romeo." She scooped up the mess, long strands of floating silky white dog hair irritating her nose. She dropped the pens back into the container. "Ivan?" Her boss held the glass coffee carafe above the mug in his hand, but instead of pouring, he stared at the empty cup as if he couldn't decide what to do next. "Want me to snoop around for anything newsworthy for next month's Christmas edition while I'm gone?" She waited, fully expecting her question to take a few seconds to get through his foggy grief.

Instead, Ivan's head snapped up, his eyes suddenly cleared. "Unless you've given any more thought to buying me out, what little bit of news you can scrape up won't be enough to matter." He chose a cup and poured the last dregs of very stout coffee into his *Mess with the Editor - End Up on the Front Page* mug. Leona had gifted him the stocking stuffer as a joke last Christmas, but she knew the saying accurately stated his reporting philosophy. One of many reasons she admired her boss.

Ivan had been a friend to her, taken a chance on her, given her a reason to get out of bed after the death of her own spouse. She owed Ivan as big as the favor he'd asked of her, but she'd also learned from experience that it was best not to make major life-changing decisions while deep in grief.

Leona wriggled into her coat. "This paper has been in your family for years. Don't you want to keep it in the family?"

"You know Hathleen and I were never blessed with children. And my sister's boys don't want to be saddled with . . ." his voice trailed, but she knew he's stopped just short of saying a dying business in a dead town. "Selling the paper to you would a feel like I was keeping it in the family." This burst of fire in Ivan was short lived. He sank into his wooden desk chair. "If it's the price that—"

"Ivan, you know I can well afford to purchase your business." Everyone in town knew of the massive fortune Leona's first husband had left her. She'd never flaunted the money and had tried to be as secretive as J.D. had been when he'd banked-rolled Cotton's investments. She did her good deeds behind closed doors. But in Mt. Hope, few things were really secret. She might as well have let Ivan print a front-page article about her charitable gifts to the hospital, college scholarship funds, and renovations to the small community church where she and J.D. had served for eighteen years . . . where her son David had taken over his father's role as pastor. Everyone knew Leona Harper Levy was an easy mark when it came to helping the good people of Mt. Hope.

"I'm not trying to make you do something you don't want to do, Leona," Ivan said. "Heaven knows you've had a lifetime of trying to live up to everyone's expectations." Ivan's coffee cup shook in his clutched hands. "It's just that you're simply the logical choice. Seemed right to give you first shot before I officially put the business on the market." He studied her, reading her as closely as he read her editorials. "If you're not interested—"

"I *am* interested. *Very* interested." The truth bubbled out like an unexpected and embarrassing burp.

She knew the power of a local newspaper to bring a community together was on the verge of being a thing of the past. But then, so was she. She'd lived her whole life in a supporting role. As the only daughter of Roberta

Worthington, she'd been the jewel in her mother's crown. As the wife of a pastor, she'd been his wingman, always flying under the radar to make sure J.D. looked good and wasn't hit by enemy fire while never calling attention to herself. In fact, both of her children had grown up to be so much like their father that she couldn't even claim them as something she'd done just for herself.

Although Ivan had taken a huge risk when he hired a reporter with no newspaper experience, her role at the *Messenger* had always been a supportive one. Granted, she'd finally worked her way up to having her own byline and had even written a few headline stories. But, truth be known, the success of the paper had never been up to her.

Ivan cleared his throat. "If you and Saul would rather retire and buy a fancy RV with an automatic slide-out porch to shade your rockin' chairs," he persisted, "I would never stand in your way."

Leona dug her purse out of her desk drawer. "Modyne and her husband tried living in one of those motorized boxes and look at her now. Back at her news desk in less than six months."

"Leave me out of this," Modyne said over her computer monitor.

"Even if Saul was ready to give up his law practice, which he isn't," Leona argued, more with herself than Ivan. "He'd never ask me to give up doing what I love. Our minds would turn to mush if all we had to do was sit in porch rockers."

"Do we have a deal then?"

All one had to do was check Facebook to know that newspapers were dying all over the country. She couldn't bear to add one more loss to her list. She'd lost J.D. She'd lost the parsonage she'd loved. She'd lost her place as the pastor's wife. She didn't want to lose friends who might have to move to the city to seek employment if this town completely dried up. And she sure didn't want to lose the purpose this job had given her life.

"How soon do you need to know?"

He opened his desk drawer and pulled out a glossy brochure. "Hathleen always wanted to see Ireland. We'd planned to go for our fortieth anniversary. I'm going to make the trip in her honor. I leave the day after Thanksgiving."

Sadness, unexpected as one of those Gulf Coast waves that had knocked her off her feet the last time she and Saul got away for a few days, hit her hard. Life didn't promise forever.

"Of course, you should go." Leona took the brochure he held out and studied the beautiful green hills. "Hathleen would have wanted you to."

He swiped at the wet streak on his cheek then sank into his chair. "You and I have always been straight with each other, right?"

"Always."

"I'm sure this will come as no surprise, but newspapers . . . well, they don't generate enough revenue to live on anymore. If you don't buy the *Messenger* . . . I'm not sure anyone will." Ivan's straight talk was his roundabout way of letting her know that if he couldn't sell his business, he'd have to walk away from his entire life's work with his bank account as empty as his heart. She knew full well, after leaving formal ministry after thirty years, how it felt to have little to show for years of effort.

"I don't know if that's true, Ivan." She handed him his brochure. "Without local journalism, who'll keep an eye on the county commissioners, or chronicle the accomplishments of Mt. Hope's school children, or write the obituary tributes of our loved ones?"

She could see him weighing his response because she'd written J.D.'s obituary, and he knew how much his unedited publication of the tribute had meant to her.

Ivan gave a woeful shake of is head. "Folks can find out that stuff on Facebook before I can even get my laptop open."

"But they can't clip out a Facebook post then stick it in their Bible," Leona argued.

"These days, most people read their Bible on their phone."

"I refuse to let you give up on this paper, or on life, Ivan Tucker."

He dropped the brochure into his desk drawer and pushed it shut. "Too late."

She couldn't turn her back on the man who'd refused to turn his back on her. The very least she could do was to make sure Ivan didn't end up living under the overpass at the edge of town. "I'll have Saul draw up the legal papers tomorrow." She stuck out her gloved hand. "Full price."

Ivan shook his head. "I can't, in good conscience, take full price."

"It's all or nothing, Ivan." Leona waved her outstretched hand. "Do we have a deal?"

A smile spread across Ivan's face. The first real smile he'd given anyone in a month. He stood and took her hand. "Deal."

With a simple handshake, Leona became the proud owner of something she could finally call her own. She looked around at the empty desks, bulging filing cabinets, and smudged windows. The tattered and threadbare newspaper business was all hers. A buzz of possibilities ignited a smile across her face.

Modyne shook her head. "Does this mean I've got a new boss?"

"I believe it does, Modyne," Ivan said. "But it's up to Leona who stays and who goes."

Modyne's gaze shot to Leona, her eyes wide with apprehension. "Do I still have a job?"

With thoughts and emotions swirling in Leona's head, it felt like she been dunked under water. "Of course, you have a job, Modyne."

"Good." Modyne went back to clicking away on her keyboard. "Then I'll write up next month's headline."

Without Ivan to run interference, she would obviously need to draw some boundaries, otherwise she'd be mowed down by Modyne. "I think *we* should discuss headlines. Work on them together."

"But this is a good one." Modyne clicked away. "It's gonna sell a bushel of papers."

"Okay," Leona sighed. "Let's hear it."

"It's printing now." Modyne reached over and snatched the paper from the printer's jaws. "Here you go." Big, bold letters splashed across the page.

"Ex-pastor's wife takes on bankrupt newspaper in dying west Texas town." Leona wadded the paper and tossed it in the trash. "Like I said, headlines will be something we tackle together."

Modyne was still cackling when Leona snatched her dog's leash and stormed out the door.

CHAPTER TWO

Leona

Romeo shot from the newspaper office and went straight for the lamppost outside Ruthie's diner. Leona struggled to keep hold of her umbrella as she waited for Romeo to relieve himself. After he'd watered the pole, his big brown eyes seemed to ask, "Now what?"

Cutting winds blew the rain sideways on the deserted street. To her right, Leona could see Ruthie hunched over her cash register like she'd just checked out a customer, but Ruthie's grandson Angus was the only other soul in the small café. Across the street, Roxie's husband pushed a broom down the customerless aisles of Brewer's Auto & Tractor Parts. Not a single patron had shopped the few remaining businesses on Main Street today. Why had she given in to Ivan? Bought a business sure to fail?

She knew why.

Her desire to leave some sort of legacy.

A gust of wind whipped the ends of her neck scarf like a surrender flag. Who was she to think she could singlehandedly take on the revival of this town?

Leona tugged Romeo's leash. "Come on, boy. I need to tell Saul what I've done before Modyne takes it upon herself to handle my marriage too." She led her dog toward the only car parked on Main Street. "We'll stop by Saul's office after we finish our rounds at the hospital."

She was fumbling in her purse for her keys when someone called, "Hey, Mrs. H . . . I mean Mrs. L."

Leona turned to see Angus waving to her from the open door of his grandmother's diner. The cold, brisk wind swept the smell of the Koffee Kup's trademark fried liver and onions past her nose. "Hey, Angus."

Ruthie's grandson had grown several inches during the four years he was away at college. He'd worked hard on his studies but gave up on taming his red hair. Thankfully, education had not erased the sprinkle of freckles across his nose, the bright twinkle in his eyes, or his love for wearing J.D.'s old suits.

"I haven't had time to stop by the paper and thank you since I got home from Europe." Deep dimples framed his smile. "If you've got time for a cup of coffee, I'm buying."

Secretly gifting this fine young man the college graduation trip of a lifetime had given her so much joy. "I want to hear all about your backpacking trip, Angus, but Romeo and I are trying to squeeze in our hospital visits before this storm cuts loose." She hated causing his smile to melt. From the moment Ruthie had taken in her grandson, Angus had done what he could to drum up business for her diner. "Tell you what, Angus. If your grandmother is okay with letting Romeo sit under the table, I'll swing by and pick up Saul after we finish our hospital rounds, then we'll stop by for a bite of dinner."

"You know MeMaw's bark is worse than her bite," Angus said. "She loves Romeo. It'll be fine."

"Your grandmother may have made her peace with sharing prime diner parking spaces with me, but she still scares me a little," Leona teased.

"Me too," Angus smiled. "But, as you can see, nobody's fighting for parking spaces these days."

"I know it's worrisome," Leona agreed. "But if you and I start praying about it, I'm sure we can come up with something, right?"

Angus flashed her an optimistic smile. "Right!"

The ever-hopeful naivete of youth was a trait she hoped life never knocked out of him. While God had proven his ability to bless her no matter how hopeless she deemed her situation, God was not a vending machine. He'd given her a job, a new husband, and a rather large nest egg for a reason. Although she was reluctant to assign motives to God, what if he'd chosen her to buy the dying newspaper in a dying town for the express purpose of turning Mt. Hope around? The idea God was calling her to make a difference was a lightning bolt she'd not felt since her days as a pastor's wife.

Limbs tingling with excitement, Leona brought Romeo into a heel. "Angus, ask Ruthie to have a couple of chicken fried steaks and a mound of mashed potatoes ready in about an hour, okay?"

He gave her a pleased thumbs-up. "I'm on it."

"Never had a doubt." Leona loaded Romeo into her SUV. Saul deserved to hear that she'd bought the newspaper from her. Best if she told him her plan to revive Mt. Hope over a steaming plate of his favorite diner foods. Guilt, prickly as a tumbleweed, rolled across her shoulders. Choosing to tell Saul what she'd done in the presence of witnesses was taking the chicken-way out. Her new husband had always been proud and supportive of her job at the *Messenger*. If he'd told her once, he'd told her a million times that he believed she could do anything she set her mind to. But she didn't want him to just humor her, she wanted him to be happy for her. To admire her business ability and writing talent. To get behind her new purpose.

Leona threw the car shifter into reverse and spun away from the curb. Would she ever shake this crippling need to have everyone's full-fledged approval? Why couldn't she be more like Roxie? Her best friend didn't give a flying flip what anyone thought about anything or anyone . . . and Roxie had no interest in changing herself to fit into anyone's mold. Would it have been any less of a leap of faith if she'd walked across the street and asked Roxie what she thought of buying the newspaper? Come to think of Roxie, she hadn't seen the flaming redhead all day. Business might be slow, but Roxie never missed a day in her shop.

Leona brushed off her concern as being overprotective. Roxie was a big girl, and she certainly didn't owe Leona a running report on her whereabouts. Leona pushed a button on the fancy dash of her new car and sent Saul a voice text that she was running up to the hospital. She would swing past his office and pick him up in about an hour.

Dinner at the diner okay with you? she asked in the voice text.

Saul immediately replied. *Storm could get bad. You sure we shouldn't head home before the bridge ices?*

She chuckled at his good-natured jab at her previous obsession. Wait until he found out her newest obsession would make the county and city officials beg for her old agenda. Such a revelation demanded the perfect setting. Mashed potatoes. Fried meat. And as many prayers as she could cram in between now and dinner at the diner.

She texted Saul. *I promised the oncology staff I'd bring Romeo by for a visit today.*

Chicken fried steak it is then. We can always grab a room at the parsonage if the roads get too bad.

She couldn't help but smile at how comfortable Saul had become with her family. He'd worked hard to make her family his family. He'd invested a great deal of time getting to know her son David. Spending hours on the lake, fishing and getting to know her boy's dreams, as well as his frustrations of being a pastor. Whenever her grandchildren spent the night, it was Saul the kids curled up with on the couch. Maddie had come to admire Saul as well. Several times since her daughter's return to the States, she mentioned that she believed Saul's business and medical insights had helped to bring Mt. Hope's hospital into the twenty-first century. Saul might grumble and make several admirable points about her hastiness, but in the end, he would come around to using her newspaper ownership to help Mt. Hope. As for the plan, she felt confident God would reveal it sooner rather than later once she had an opportunity to explain the urgency to him.

Leona tossed her phone into her purse. "See, Romeo," she said to the giant ball of hair perched in the front seat. "Everything's going to be just fine."

Rain doused the few cars in the hospital parking lot. Saul was right. This storm was shaping up to be a doozy. Perhaps the non-essential staff could be released early. She'd keep her visit short, and if the weather had worsened by the time she finished, she and Saul could pick up the chicken fried steaks on their way home. Angus would understand if she had to delay their much-needed catch-up.

Leona wheeled into a space close to the front entrance. Lifting her coat collar against the sting of rain, she helped Romeo from her SUV. "Let's go to work, boy."

Romeo's tail swished happily as he pulled her along the slick sidewalk. The hospital's automatic door slid open. An antiseptic-smelling warmth hit Leona's face. Romeo shook the rain from his silky coat. Leona removed her gloves.

"Leona!" The Story twins waved to her from behind the sleek new welcome desk, their gray perms wound tight and their smiles wide.

"Hey, Etta May. Nola Gay." She waved a wet glove at the elderly sisters. There had been quite the discussion in the HR department as to whether it was too much of a liability for the hospital to let two ninety-year-olds push the magazine cart. In the end, Leona had managed to pull strings and the sisters had been granted a once-a-week gig sitting at the welcome desk. "You girls staying out of trouble?"

Nola Gay wheeled her desk chair away from the huge computer monitor. "Do weevils cause stem rot?"

"Why yes they do," Leona chuckled.

"Then you have your answer." Etta May slipped a stack of tri-fold brochures into a clear holder on the counter. "You here to check on Roxie?"

"Roxie?" Leona didn't think Etta May looked confused, but the question Etta May had just asked didn't make sense. Leona tried to gently steer the old woman back on course. "I haven't seen Roxie all day. But she's probably in the back of her shop taking inventory."

Nola Gay shook her head. "We saw her slip in the side door a couple of hours ago." She pointed toward the adjoining hall. "Kept her head down, but those long legs are hard to hide in a short skirt."

Romeo let out a big bark and lunged. The leash flew out of Leona's hand. Before she could recover her hold, her dog had his paws planted on Roxie's shoulders and he was happily licking her face.

"Roxie?" Leona stood immobile trying to figure out why her friend had been so secretive. "You didn't tell me you were coming to the hospital. Did you have a doctor's appointment?"

The fiery redhead cut a disapproving look toward the old twins peering over their matching glasses. "Leona, get this throw rug off me." Roxie did an uncharacteristic two-step backup, her chin lifted and her mascara-streaked face turned toward Leona in an effort to avoid Romeo's big wet tongue. "Call off your dog."

"Sorry." Leona scrambled for the trailing leash. "Romeo, down."

The dog dropped to all fours and hung his head as if he didn't understand why the only person who adored him as much as he worshipped Leona wasn't glad to see him.

"I'm sorry, Roxie." Leona wrestled Romeo back to her side. "You know how much he loves you."

Roxie plucked at the dog hair clinging to her short, pencil skirt. "Hell's bells, Leona. I'll have to send this entire outfit to the cleaners."

Leona cocked her head, trying to figure out why her usually bubbly friend let a dog push her out of sorts. "Send *me* the bill."

"The auto parts business may not be great, but I can still pay for my own dry cleaning." Roxie adjusted the purse strap slung over her shoulder. "Hang on to him and let me go close up my store." She charged past.

"Wait a minute." Leona snagged her friend's coat. "What's wrong?"

"It's getting late, and I need to help Tom close before . . ." Roxie's angry voice trailed off.

"Before what?"

"Before I tell him."

Leona handed Romeo's leash over to Nola Gay. She turned and took Roxie by the elbow. "Come with me."

Roxie dug in with her three-inch heels. "Leona, I need to go. Tom's gonna be worried sick."

"You're in no shape to drive," Leona argued. "I've got four-wheel drive. Text Tom and tell him I'm taking you back to your store."

"What about my car?"

"We'll get your car later."

"I may not have later." Roxie looked her square in the eye. "I've got cancer, Leona."

CHAPTER THREE

Leona

Nola Gay and Etta May were too busy activating the prayer chain to notice that Leona had retrieved Romeo's leash and taken her friend by the hand.

"Let's go, Roxie."

Icy rain shards cut into the hot tears coming down Leona's face as she and Roxie walked arm-in-arm across the parking lot. Terrifying questions created a log jam in Leona's tightening throat. Roxanne Brewer was her best friend in the world. If it hadn't been for Roxie in the days following J.D.'s death, she'd still be cowering in bed with the covers pulled over her head. She couldn't just stay mute. She had to say something comforting.

"What did Dr. Boyer say exactly, Roxie?" squeaked past the lump in her throat.

"I need to go to Dallas to see a specialist." Roxie stumbled, but Leona didn't let her fall.

"We can ask Maddie who she'd recommend."

"Dr. Boyer refused to guess the stage. Says I'll need a lumpectomy ASAP at the very least."

"Get in." Leona clicked the auto start and the locks on the SUV popped up. "Romeo can ride in the back."

Leona closed the dog safely in the kennel she kept in the back then slid in behind the wheel. "I'll take you home and we'll make a plan."

"Take me to the store." Roxie dug a tube of lipstick and a tissue from her purse, flipped the visor mirror, then started scrubbing at the black trails of makeup on her cheeks. "Tom needs to hear this from me. Not one of those loose-lipped hussies on the Storys' prayer chain." She ran a fresh coat of burnt amber over her trembling lips.

Leona let Roxie's disdain for the Storys and their efforts to do good works slide. Roxie loved these two old women as much as she. This unusual sniping meant her friend was more worried than she wanted to let on.

"You're right. Best if Tom hears it from you." Car heater blaring, Leona headed toward Brewer's Auto & Tractor Parts. The sky had turned as dark as the fog of uncertainties rolling over her. "They've got all sorts of treatments now. Just the other day I saw on Facebook where a woman was celebrating fifteen years cancer free."

"Hell's bells, Leona." Roxie flipped the visor up. "You know you can't believe everything you read on Facebook." She stuffed the tissue and lipstick in her purse then pulled the giant Louis Vuitton knock-off close to her chest. "Slow down. I'm not dying yet."

Die? Leona gripped the steering wheel, panic pounding in her ears. "Of course, you're not..." If she said the word, she might melt into a puddle. Falling apart would not help Roxie.

Once they reached the parts store, Leona eased into one of the many the empty slots. She and Roxie sat in silence watching the windshield wipers swat the rain that had morphed into sticky little sleet pellets. Florescent lights from inside the business Roxie and Tom had built with their bare hands cast a blue tint on the icy sidewalk. Not another person was in the store. Maybe no one had come in all day. Tom, a handsome man with a shiny bald crown, was head-down at the register. Probably counting every nickel and wondering how they were going to keep the lights on. Gone were the days when he and Roxie could have sold their business for a tidy profit and retired on a beach in Florida. Tom would be as lost as Ivan if he lost Roxie.

Suddenly saving the town seemed unimportant. Saving Roxie was all that mattered.

Stop it, Leona Levy! Don't let your mind go anywhere near the negative.

Leona turned toward the woman who'd made a career out of being everyone's rock. Roxie's four children adored her. Her husband Tom worshipped the ground she walked on. Leona's own two kids called Roxie their Aunt Roxie. And Leona knew, no matter what, she could count on Roxie to always have her back.

Roxie stared straight ahead, her watery eyes not blinking. How could someone who was hugging fifty-five not have a single wrinkle? Even more impressive...how did someone remain so stoic as they prepared to relay such horrible news to the person they'd loved the most for nearly thirty-five years?

Leona took and breath and whispered, "Want me to go in with you?"

Roxie swallowed hard. "This is something I have to do . . . alone."

Leona grabbed Roxie's hand. "We're in this together, and we're going to beat it."

Roxie turned her beautiful face to Leona. Her lips were drawn into a stiff smile, but the fire in those don't-mess-with-me-eyes was barely a flicker. "You bet your boots, girlfriend." She leaned over, kissed Leona on the cheek, then swung her long legs out into the cold.

The rhythmic swipe of the wipers made it seem like she was watching the scene inside the hardware store from outside a shaken snow globe. Tom heard the bell above the door when Roxie walked in.

Swipe.

He looked up from the cash register.

Swipe.

He took one look at her, and his smile slid from his face.

Swipe.

Leona could see that he was listening to whatever Roxie had decided to tell him.

Swipe.

While she was still talking, he dropped what little cash they'd made that week and flew around the counter.

Swipe.

In one giant swoop, he wrapped Roxie in his arms.

Fresh tears watered Leona's dormant grief. How many times had she asked herself what she would have done had she been given any warning that she was losing J.D.? She told herself she'd have dropped everything and rushed to save him. Truth was, she'd been given plenty of warning. But she'd been so busy trying to be everything to everyone, she missed the signs. J.D. had been complaining of exhaustion for weeks and she'd just sloughed it off as needing a vacation. Why hadn't she insisted he see a doctor? Watching Tom melt into a puddle, she realized that knowing exactly what was beyond today wasn't always a blessing.

Leona's cell rang over her car speaker. The name on the caller ID glowed *Saul*. She'd been so immersed in her friend's troubles she'd forgotten her promise to her husband.

She rubbed at the tears pouring down her face. Crying had never changed a thing and yet she couldn't seem to stop. "Saul."

"Leona, are you okay?" The frantic edge in Saul's usually controlled voice pumped more tears down her cheeks. "Nola Gay just called."

"It's not good, Saul."

"We're not going to borrow trouble. You hear me, Leona?"

"Can you call Ruthie and cancel our dinner order? I don't feel much like chicken fried steak tonight."

"Sure." The start of his car came over the speaker. "Where are you? I'll come to you."

"Brewers Auto. I couldn't let Roxie drive."

"Was she in bad shape?"

"I think she's still in shock."

"Sounds like you are too. Stay put. I'm coming."

She and Saul did not experience love at first sight. In fact, their prickly working relationship had required lots of coaxing to get past the pain of lost loves. Compared to her laid-back first husband, Saul was wound tight. Compared to Saul's successful first wife Claire, Leona felt she would never measure up, not that Saul ever compared her to Claire. It was a comparison of her own making, her nasty tendency to worry about what others thought of her.

Saul had relaxed considerably since they married. She'd worked to gain more confidence and to embrace the freedom Saul had granted her to go her own way. Do her own thing. Break out from the judgment she'd always felt heaped upon her by her mother and then by the fine folks at Mt. Hope Community Church. But tonight, she was glad to have someone telling her what to do.

"Saul?"

"I'm on my way, sweetheart."

"I love you, Saul Levy."

Chapter Four

Ruthie

Ruthie Crouch stuffed the eviction notice under the empty change drawer in her cash register. Forty years of her life devoted to this diner and all she had to show for her efforts were empty booths and fallen arches. She'd dreamed of owning The Koffee Kup since the first time she'd shared a root beer float and dreamed up recipes with Earl Dean Crouch in the back booth. As he scribbled their ideas on napkins, their passion for cooking ignited a sizzling hot forbidden love.

Despite her daddy's warning to stay away from the drifter he'd hired to cook for his cattle hands during branding season, the day she turned eighteen, she and Earl hitched a ride to Abilene and got married. Instead of hopping from one restaurant to the next like Earl suggested, her guilt got the better of her and she told Earl she needed to go home and make amends with her daddy. Earl reluctantly agreed to return to Mt. Hope on the condition she wouldn't expect him to work for her daddy the rest of his life. It only took spending a couple of nights in her parents' home to talk him into signing a year-to-year lease on the diner, move into the diner's upstairs apartment, and set to work turning the greasy space into a fine dining establishment—a big first for a small west Texas oil town.

They'd only been married six weeks when Ruth discovered she was pregnant. Two days later, the army drafted Earl to fight in Vietnam.

After spending seven months overseas, Earl acquired a bad limp and a medical discharge. The skittish chain smoker who got off that discharge bus was not the same starry-eyed dreamer she'd married. His leg hurt him bad, she could tell, but it had enough get-up-and-go left in it to carry him out of town less than a month after his homecoming. She hadn't seen Earl since he up and left her with nothing but a bun in the oven and keys to this diner.

Determined to show her daddy she could keep her baby fed and a roof over her head, Ruthie added blue-plate specials and homemade pies to the diner's menu. Soon every roughneck in the county bellied up to her counter for breakfast, lunch, and dinner. Her profit margin was small, but she'd managed to make enough in tips to raise her Ruby. Before her daddy died, he'd told her he was proud of her.

Ruthie had barely gotten her daddy's headstone set when history repeated itself. Her Ruby, newly turned eighteen and tired of Ruthie's rules, stormed out of the diner one rainy night. It wasn't until the next morning that Ruthie learned Ruby had run off with a long-haul trucker. For sixteen long, lonely years, Ruthie hoped against hope that Ruby would come home. Then one day, an underfed and homeless teenager named Angus showed up on her doorstep and delivered the shocking news that he was her grandson and that his mother Ruby had died a few months back. Ruthie, both heartbroken and overjoyed, had taken one look at the boy and knew the Lord had given her a second chance.

Ruthie glanced at the handsome redhead talking on the phone while firing up the grill. Her Angus was twenty-two now. Ever the loyal one. He had been no more than a child of sixteen when he'd nursed his dying mother—right up to the ugly end. Ruthie had no doubt he would stay to care for her. No matter how ugly it got.

After what she'd been through with Earl and Ruby, Ruthie valued loyalty and commitment to family above all else, but she'd relied on this young man's steadfastness long enough. She'd learned the hard way that loyalty could also be a ball and chain. A weight so heavy it could drown dreams.

Angus had been offered several jobs that promised to utilize his college business degree. But he refused to leave her to die alone in this dying town. Much as she dreaded the thought of finishing her twilight years without her grandson's constant companionship, she wanted to encourage her precious boy to reach for the stars. And she needed to do it before his undying devotion sentenced him to a life stuck behind a diner counter.

Getting more customers in the door would set her business right and hopefully put his mind at ease.

Angus hung up the phone. "That was Saul. He asked me to keep an eye on Leona until he can get here."

"I saw her leave the newspaper office thirty minutes ago."

"He says she's at Brewers." Angus went to the diner window. "Yep, that's her car. Wonder why she parked in front of Roxie's store?" He turned to Ruthie. "Saul said Leona got some bad news, so they'll be picking up those chicken friend steaks to go."

Ruthie let her gaze slide to Leona's shiny SUV. What did that woman have to worry about? Her first husband had left her a fortune and her second husband had a thriving law practice and plenty of money of his own. Leona's two grown children would make any mother proud. David was doing a respectable job filling his deceased father's pulpit, and Maddie had made it home safe and sound from saving the world on the mission field.

Ruthie would be the first to admit that she and Leona had had their differences, but they'd made their peace, especially since she was sure it was Leona Levy who'd secretly made it financially possible for Angus to attend college. Back when Leona first got hired on at The *Messenger*, she'd been wrong to insist Leona not park her old van in front of the diner, and she'd long since told her so. But Angus was right. It was strange to see Leona's new SUV parked across the street instead of her usual spot.

"I'll get their dinner plated." Ruthie shuffled to the counter. "Hope the bad news has nothing to do with David or Maddie. Leona dotes on those two kids of hers."

"You dote on me, MeMaw."

She pinched his cheek. "Grandmothers can't help it."

Angus grinned. "Well, David was fine when he came in for our Bible study this morning." Angus handed her a to-go box. "He said Maddie and Parker were still settling in, but glad to be back home in Mt. Hope."

"Look." Ruthie pointed to Roxie's sudden appearance at Leona's car window. "Can you tell what Roxie's saying?"

Angus hurried back to the window. "Looks like Roxie's telling Mrs. L to move along."

"Leona and Roxie are best friends." Ruthie bagged up an extra helping of mashed potatoes. "I'm headin' over to check on Roxie after Saul and Leona pick up their dinner. If Brewers is fixin' to close their doors . . ." she didn't finish what she was thinking, but one look at Angus told her he was as worried as she that they were about to be the last business standing.

Chapter Five

Leona

"You sit." Saul led Leona to the couch that faced the windows showcasing their lakefront view. "I'll start a fire."

Leona sank into the overstuffed couch. "Saul?"

"Just rest, sweetheart. You've had a shock." With military precision, her husband laid the logs and lit a match. Firelight soon danced in the darkened room.

She knew she'd intended to talk to Saul about something important during dinner, but whatever it was had disappeared behind the black cloud of Roxie's diagnosis.

"I'll change." Saul patted her hand. "Then dish up the chicken fried steaks."

"I'm not hungry."

"You're going to need to keep your strength up if you're going to help Roxie."

"Help her?" Leona blinked back tears. "She made it very clear that this is a battle she'll have to fight on her own."

"We'll talk about how to best help Roxie after I get some chow in you."

"She's stubborn, you know."

"Fortunately, I am experienced in dealing with stubborn women." Saul kissed her forehead. "Rest."

Leona settled back into the thick cushions, slipped her feet out of her boots, snagged the woolen throw, then draped the blanket around her shoulders. With each crack and pop of the oak logs, she curled deeper into herself. The day J.D. died, it was Roxie who'd wrapped her in a crocheted throw and held her together. When she didn't know where she was going to live or how she would support herself, it was Roxie who'd believed in her. When it seemed as if she'd failed to put her family back together, Roxie stood beside her and refused to let her give up.

Saul was right. Somehow, someway, she had to find the strength to return the favor. Roxie didn't deserve as good a friend as she'd been, she deserved better.

Weariness settled so heavy on Leona that she let her eyelids close. The next thing she knew, Saul was gently shaking her shoulder.

"How about I put Ruthie's chicken fried steaks in the fridge and scramble some eggs?" Saul had changed out of his starched white shirt and slacks with their sharp military crease. His flannel pajama bottoms and military old sweatshirt had been carefully chosen to give him the appearance of comfort and safety, but the worry she'd heard in his voice when she'd told him about Roxie's cancer had crept into his eyes. Breast cancer were two words this dear man knew all too well. He'd cared for his first wife through her slow and painful struggle with the disease.

Leona pressed against the couch and tried to stand. "I can help with dinner."

"Stay put." He tucked the throw around her neck. "A cup of decaf might put a stop to this shivering."

"Saul," Leona said, her teeth chattering. "I bought the Messenger this afternoon."

His eyes studied hers with that way of his that made her feel he could see deep into her soul. "Well, you've had quite the day."

"I didn't talk to you about it when Ivan first mentioned it to me because . . . because I thought his offer to sell it to me was just his grief talking. It's easy to make impulsive decisions during grief. I thought that once the fog began to lift, he'd change his mind about letting go of his family business. Then today, when he asked me again, I could see he was just so desperate to leave behind anything that reminded him of his life with his dear wife that I made him a spontaneous offer."

"Spontaneous?" Saul's grin broke into a huge smile. "You, the woman who starts planning next year's Christmas dinner in January, did something spontaneous?"

"Why is that so funny? I've had to learn to be flexible."

"Leona," Saul sat beside her and drew her close. "You can think on your feet better than anyone I know."

"Then why did I let myself get carried away by Ivan's sob story?"

"Tell yourself whatever you must, but buying Ivan out wasn't really *all* that spontaneous."

"What's that supposed to mean?"

"First of all, everything you love is right here in this town. Your kids. Your church. Your friends."

"You," she added.

"Especially me," he paused and let out a sigh, "But here's the real truth."

"The real truth."

"I don't believe the decision to own your dream was the least bit impulsive."

"My dream?"

"You've always wanted to explore who you really are. Owning your own business and writing whatever you want whenever you want has been your prayer for years. God never forgets the desires of our hearts."

"If that's the case, then I'm reminding God of how much I desire to have my friend Roxie around for a long time."

Saul kissed her cheek. "Attagirl!"

Headlights swept through the living room. "Who'd come out in this weather?"

Saul went to the window and peered out. "The best pastor in town."

"I'm going to box the ears of that crazy boy of mine." Leona flung the blanket from her shoulders. "David Harper," She growled as she opened the front door. "I should tan your hide. What were you thinking coming out in this weather?"

David ignored Leona's insistence that he turn around this very minute and hightail it back to his family. "Momma, I came to discuss the Christmas Eve service."

"Christmas is weeks away. You could have called."

"I could have."

"But the truth is?" she waited while David shifted from foot to foot.

"Roxie means the world to me, too."

Cold night air swirled around Leona. "Let me guess, the Story sisters phoned you."

"They mean well, Momma."

She and David were silent for a moment, David's breath cloudy in the porch light as she processed how Roxie would react to everyone in town knowing her business.

Saul was the one who ended the stalemate. "You two bring your fight inside. I've need to get dinner on the stove, and I don't have the bandwidth to cook and referee."

Fifteen minutes later, the three of them huddled close to the fire with plates of scrambled eggs and toast balanced on their knees. Together, they talked about how to best support Tom and Roxie as they walked this difficult road.

David shoveled in the last of his eggs. "Next to you, Momma, Roxie is the toughest woman I know."

God deserved the credit for the way her son had come to admire her, but David's improved opinion of her abilities was recently acquired and not necessarily set in stone.

"I bought the *Messenger* today." Leona clasped a warm mug of decaf coffee, watching the news pull her son's features into disapproval.

"You did what?"

"I didn't sell a kidney." Leona sipped her decaf. "I simply bought a business."

"Momma, it's just ..."

"It's just what?" Leona insisted. "More than you think I can handle?"

David shook his head. "Newspapers are a dying breed."

"Print journalism is lagging," Leona admitted, refusing to let David rain on her parade. "But I have plans."

"Plans?"

"Plans to revitalize the newspaper business in order to revitalize this town."

"What kind of plans?"

Her own goals and dreams to leave a mark on the world suddenly seemed rather shallow in light of Roxie's unsettling future, but for some reason she could not back down. "I'm going to make some updates. Paint the place. Seek more advertisers. Add a digital edition." She had no idea why she'd just spouted that absurd proposition. She'd never been a fan of digital news. Like people who preferred paperbacks to ereaders, she loved the weight of importance ink and processed pulp added to the community's recent and upcoming events. Digital news felt weightless, unanchored, and distant.

"Momma, the digital world is—"

"Above my pay grade?"

He shook his head. "Your computer skills have come a long way since you started at the paper." David was quickly becoming the same skilled peacemaker his father had been. "I'm just saying, saving a newspaper is going to take a monumental effort."

Her inability to acquire this highly prized virtue irritated her greatly, but not as much as her lagging computer skills. No matter how hard she worked to understand the different computer programs, anything more than working in WORD or answering emails still threw her for a loop. "Well, what I can't do on my own, I'll hire out."

"Who are you going to hire?"

"I don't know *who*, David." Leona stood and took her son's empty plate. "But I'm sure the Lord and I can figure it out."

"Look, Momma." David rose. "It's your money, to do with as you wish. But—"

"Don't waste what your father worked so hard for but never got to enjoy?" She could see that she'd hurt him, and she hated it when she let her undealt-with emotions of the day get the better of her. She was mad at the injustices of this life...the injustices of Roxie's diagnosis. Not her son, or his willingness to speak truth.

"Roxie's at the top of our prayer list." David kissed her cheek. "If we can do anything to help her and Tom, you know we will."

"David," Leona swallowed the fear gathering in her throat. Fear that her savvy son was right. She had bitten off more than she could chew by taking on the newspaper. But the possibility of losing a few thousand dollars was not the fear that had hounded her all the way home from the auto parts store. Life was so short. Hers included. Whether or not she ever accomplished her dreams mattered little compared to doing what she could for Roxie.

"Give the kids a kiss for me, David."

"Always do." Her son picked up his coat and headed for the door then turned. "Momma, you've already proven to everyone in this town that you can do anything you set your mind to. I have no doubt that you can run a newspaper with the same efficiency and success you used to run the church's ladies' ministry. If you still need to prove something to yourself, then I'm behind you."

She reached up and wrapped his scarf around his neck. When had her little boy become a tower of insight and wisdom? Tucking him in brought back memories of early winter storms and ...an idea suddenly hit her hard. "David Harper, you're brilliant."

"What did I say?"

"This town." Leona ran to the dining table and started rummaging through the stack of old papers she'd promised Saul she would purge before they married. "It's in here somewhere."

"What are you looking for, Leona?" Saul joined her.

"A way to kill two birds with one stone." She found the tattered file and held it up victoriously. "David, do you want to help Roxie and me and every other business in this town stay afloat?"

"You know I do, Momma."

"Then call Angus and ask if we can have a city council meeting at the diner first thing tomorrow morning." Hope surged through her. "I'll email the council members." She waved the file at the confusion on both Saul and David's faces. "We're going to resurrect the annual Christmas parade."

Saul looked at David and shrugged. "From the gleam in her eyes, there's no sense trying to talk her out of this."

"Heaven help us," David said.

"Roads are slick tonight," Leona said, clutching the file close to her chest. "Promise me you'll be careful going over the bridges, David."

He looked deep into her eyes. "Promise me you'll ask the Lord's opinion of your plan before breakfast.

"I love you, David Harper."

"Does this mean I can still count on your help with the church's Christmas Eve program?"

Leona swatted his arm with the file folder. "Civic work will never take priority over my work for the Lord."

"Any way the church's Christmas Even service could get a front-page plug?" he asked. "We're still kind of digging out from under the pot brownie fiasco."

"You're free to submit your story idea the same as anyone else."

"See," David smiled like he'd just beat her at checkers. "You *are* a tough business woman."

Chapter Six

Ruthie

Having a little breakfast business was the only reason Ruthie had not chewed Angus out when he told her he'd agreed to David Harper's request to let the town council use the Koffee Kup's dining room for an early morning breakfast meeting.

Shoulders squared, Ruthie hurried over to her old Bunn brewer and pulled the pot of stout coffee off the burner. She'd cut corners somewhere else before she cut out her free-refill policy.

"Awful early in the season for ice, but if the temps keep dropping this rain could turn stick." Ruthie held up the pot of hot coffee. "You all need a warmup before you head out?" The skeletal remains of the town council that huddled around two dining tables pushed together ignored her hint that it was time to move on.

From what she'd overheard, they were too late when it came to searching for ways to save this town. Several Main Street businesses had already closed their doors. She hoped no one knew she was three months behind on her rent and on the verge of closing up herself.

Last week, her landlord crushed her hopes of riding out this dry spell. She thought the man she'd served free coffee and pie nearly every day for forty years had simply stopped in for his usual mid-morning snack. Took that coward until he'd swallowed the last flaky crumb of her apple crisp to work up the courage to say she had until Christmas to pay up or turn in her keys. Guess the eviction notice she received yesterday meant her offer of an extra scoop of ice cream had not changed his mind.

Leona waved from the head of the table. "I'm happy to give you a hand, Ruthie."

Leona Levy meant well, a hold-over trait from all her years as a pastor Harper's wife, but she could wear a body down with her need to help. And calling this early-morning council meeting in the middle of a rare November ice storm was a prime example. It was too late to revive Main Street. Mt. Hope was already well on its way to becoming another West Texas ghost town.

"Don't need no help." Ruthie caught the flash of disapproval Angus shot her way from his place at grill and softened her response. "But thanks anyway, Leona."

She and Angus had had this discussion about her stubborn pride many times since his return from his college years in Abilene. She wished she had a nickel for every time he said, "MeMaw, your bad back and fallen arches won't let you fry chicken livers and flip burgers forever." But wishing for money to fall out of the sky was as futile as wishing Angus would quit worrying about her. Some things just weren't going to happen.

"I got this, MeMaw." Angus gave her a wearisome shake of his head, then snatched the carafe of tar-black brew from her hand. "Refills comin' right up, Mrs. L."

Giving the town council a free meeting place was just one of many crazy notions Angus brought home from college. She'd allowed him to build the diner a Facebook business page because he claimed not having a social media presence was like wasting the gift of free advertising. She'd even pulled a twenty-dollar bill from her sock drawer so Angus could laminate the menus. But when she learned Angus had offered to toss in a free breakfast for the council members without talking to her, the extravagance had nearly pushed her right out of her orthotics.

"Keep an eye on the sugar packets, Angus," Ruthie whispered. "I ain't Santa Claus."

Angus's face went red as his hair. He bent his six-foot-two frame until his embarrassed breath grazed her good ear, "Goodwill is a good thing."

"Goodwill," Ruthie muttered as she shuffled to the grill. "Angus Dean Freestone, you're going to *goodwill* us right out of house and home."

Angus grabbed a handful of silverware bundles wrapped in paper napkins. "I came back to Mt. Hope to help you the way you helped me, and that's exactly what I intend to do."

Ruthie flipped flapjacks big as her swollen ankles onto dinner plates. If she told Angus how close she was to losing the diner, he'd never leave her. Much as that selfish thought gave her a great deal of comfort, keeping the diner doors open was her problem. Not his.

'Course Angus was nobody's fool. He didn't need a college degree to know that no customers meant no money in the till.

"I can't afford to keep doling out free grub," she confessed in a low whisper meant just for his ears.

He smiled like he considered it progress she'd finally admitted the obvious. "After the council's plan revitalizes Main Street, this place will be packed again."

This boy's eternal optimism was an infuriating trait he'd inherited from a man he'd never met. A man who'd promised to give her the stars, but instead broke her heart.

She'd done her best to keep Angus from floating on moonbeams, but apparently the strands of DNA that made him loyal as a golden retriever had gotten twisted with an unfortunate strand of pipe dreams.

She laid down her spatula and stared him straight in the eye. "Young man, you're not hearing me. Mt. Hope is on its last leg."

"Mrs. L and I don't believe that."

"Mrs. L doesn't have a dog in this fight."

"She does," Angus said. "I heard her announce to the council that she bought the paper from Ivan yesterday."

"Why on earth would she do such a fool thing?"

"MeMaw, you're not the only one who has dreams."

"And look where it's got me." She cocked her head toward the civic-minded freeloaders. "You should have checked with me before you gave out free breakfast vouchers."

He kissed her cheek. "You've always said I have a head for business."

"I believe I said you're too smart for your own good."

Angus smiled. "The least we can do is listen to what Mrs. L has to say."

Ruthie let her gaze slide over to Leona. The woman did seem extra wound up and more determined than ever to have her way. "Sayin' something don't make it so. It's the doing."

"Give her a chance, MeMaw. That's all I ask." He set off to deliver the coffee and silverware.

As Angus wove through the empty chairs and tables, Ruthie noticed how much her boy had changed in the four years he'd been away at school. He was no longer the gangly teenager who'd walked all the way from Maine after he was orphaned at sixteen. He was a man now. A man who filled out the old tweed sport coat he'd bought at Leona's garage sale the day she finally cleaned out her dead husband's suits. Angus was every bit as kind and generous as the pastor who used to wear that jacket. And he was far more forgiving than she had ever been, especially considering the many struggles life had thrown his way.

Oh, how she loved this young man. Had tried to do right by him from the moment he stumbled into her life. She couldn't help but feel his sudden appearance meant she'd been given a second chance, an unexpected opportunity to atone for the mistakes she'd made while singlehandedly raising her daughter. 'Course, Ruby had been headstrong and wild as a range pony. No one could have tied that beautiful girl to a two-bit diner.

"Ruthie!" Leona waved her over. "We'd love to have you join us."

"Got nothing new to add." Ruthie pointed at the chalkboard. She'd reduced prices on every blue-plate special by a dollar. "Short of handing out free pieces of pie, I've tried everything I know to do to bring in customers."

"Free pie isn't a bad idea," Howard Davis said as he stuffed another bite of syrupy pancakes in his mouth.

Ruthie jammed her balled fists atop her plump hips. "I'll start giving out free pie when you start giving out free trucks, Howard Davis."

The bald-headed, jug-eared, used-car salesman nearly choked. "I'm just—"

"Thinking about your own bottom line...as usual," Ruthie snapped.

"MeMaw, please." Angus wedged a chair between Leona and David. Then Angus patted the top of the chair, an invitation for Ruthie to swallow a bit of her pride and come sit.

Clearly, Angus was trying to save her from putting her foot in her mouth once again, but she was in no mood to be saved. "Sitting around chawing on what's wrong with the Mt. Hope economy won't get anyone anywhere. We need to *do* something."

"You're right, Ruthie," David said. "That's why Momma has suggested we resurrect the Christmas parade." David Harper had been coming to this diner to have a Saturday morning pre-fishing breakfast with his father long before he was able to see over the counter. She'd been slipping him extra helpings of hash browns for years. After his father died and David became the new pastor of Mt. Hope Community church, she'd started slipping into the pew on Sunday mornings. David reached for his mother's hand. "Right, Momma?"

Ruthie's gaze darted from David to Leona. The fashionably dressed recently remarried widow swallowed hard, but nodded agreement with her son.

Ruthie's affinity for Leona had grown considerably after Leona unexpectedly lost her husband. Leona had proved she was not the kind of woman who sat around moping. With nothing more than thirty years as a pastor's wife on her resume, she'd landed a job at the newspaper. Wasn't long before Ivan Tucker, the owner of the *Mt. Hope Messenger*, promoted her from obituary writing to reporting on the town council. And it wasn't long after Leona's first front-page article came out that the mayor promoted her to executive chairman of the city council. In the middle of all Leona's ladder climbing, she'd married a military lawyer, and did it all without losing her smile. In the eyes of this community, Leona Harper Levy had risen from the ashes wearing wings.

But the tears welling in Leona's eyes proved what Ruthie had known for years. Successfully picking yourself up was no guarantee that you stopped missing what could have been.

"David," Ruthie said, kind as she could. "The parade won't be the same without your daddy."

The parade had not been held since the year J.D. Harper dropped dead in the pulpit right before Thanksgiving. No one had the heart to step in and take J.D.'s place as Santa. Not even David. And that bright young man had done a wonderful job stepping into so many of the different shoes J.D. had worn in this town. But even David had drawn the line when it came to putting on the Santa suit and taking his father's beloved place on the decorated hay wagon pulled by a John Deere tractor.

Leona stiffened in her seat. "J.D. would have wanted us to move on, Ruthie." Her trademark composure had snapped into place. "If we're going to get this Christmas parade organized, I'm going to need all hands on deck."

Ruthie turned to Angus who nudged her with a hopeful nod.

She wiped her hands on her apron. "Guess it wouldn't hurt to get off my feet until I have a paying customer." Coffee cup in hand, she lumbered to the chair Angus had saved for her.

"Hells Bells, Ruthie," Roxie Brewer, the short-skirted owner of the auto and tractor parts store across the street had been uncharacteristically quiet this morning, especially when Ruthie asked her why she and Tom closed early last night. "You've been in business longer than any of us," Roxie went on. "If we can't learn from you, who else is there?" Those dark circles under Roxie's eyes were new too. Maybe, Ruthie thought, she wasn't the only one tossing and turning at night.

Sinking into the chair, Ruthie let her weary gaze take in those circled around her table.

Howard Davis had managed to keep his car dealership afloat by switching his inventory from new Cadillacs to used pickups. Roxie Brewer had cornered what was left of the farmers' trade when she expanded her auto parts business to include tractor parts. The Story spinsters, Etta May and Nola Gay, had taken to bending the ears of their Uber customers with gardening advice for a price and selling homemade dill pickles from the back of their van. Wayne Darling, the pasty-skinned funeral director, had made a tidy sum peddling burial plots.

And then there was Ivan Tucker, the *Mt. Hope Messenger's* previous owner. He'd lowered the cost of newspaper advertising in hopes of generating enough income to pay his wife's medical bills. Not a month went by that Ivan didn't write a front-page article about the need for everyone to support the local businesses. And he'd farmed out the paper's printing to save on costs. All those moves were risky. But this recent sale of his family's legacy proved to Ruthie that risks are called risks for a reason.

Besides, everyone at this table knew that even if she'd wanted to take some risks, she'd never had the luxury of taking them and probably never would. "Don't follow in my tracks," she said finally.

Ivan leaned forward. "All of us are struggling."

"Were struggling," Ruthie pointed out.

"Fair enough," Ivan said. "But surely you can see the value in what Leona's trying to do here."

"Sad news didn't sell enough newspapers for you to keep going, Ivan. What makes you think printing up a bunch of it will fill seats around my tables?" Ruthie ignored the laser stare of disbelief Angus aimed between her eyes and gulped a hot sip from her mug.

"Ruthie's right." Leona pushed aside her plate of untouched flapjacks. "That's why I'm proposing we give the folks in this county some *good* news." She pulled a stack of papers from her big reporter's satchel. "These parade plans are from several years ago." Leona passed out copies of the neatly typed list. "As you can see, we had the rodeo queen seated atop one of Howard's convertibles to start the parade."

"Leona," Howard wiped syrup from his chin. "I don't have many calls for fancy cars anymore. You know I had to quit stocking them."

"You've adapted, Howard," Leona corrected. "And so must Mt. Hope. The column on the left side of the page shows how the parade committee used to do things. The column on the right contains my suggested changes for this year's parade."

Howard ran a long, bony finger down the column. "You want the rodeo queen to ride a real horse?"

"Not just any horse, Howard. I want our Queen to ride one of her daddy's *best* horses."

"That's a lot of clean up." Howard dragged his palm over his bald head. "Why don't we just stack a few bales of hay in the back of one of my newer-used F150s?"

"Since the oil business has pulled out, we're a farm and ranch community now, Howard," Leona explained with the skill of a woman who had years of experience trying to bring the chairman of the church's elder board around to her way of thinking. "The more we can include actual farmers and ranchers in this event, the more likely they and their families are to make the effort to come to town."

"I know," Nola Gay clapped her hands. "Let's invite anyone with a horse to ride along with the rodeo queen," she said. "That should bring the ranchers in by the trailer load."

"Brilliant!" Leona jotted the suggestion. "Any ideas on how to get the farmers to town?"

"Tractor races down Main Street?" Howard's pouty tone sizzled with sarcasm.

At the mention of tractors, Roxie seemed to perk up. "Actually, that's not a bad idea, Howard. I could offer a free tractor tune-up to the winner."

Leona beamed. "Perfect, Roxie." As Leona put a check by Brewer Auto Parts and moved down the list, Ruthie decided she was making it a priority to find out what was going on between Leona and Roxie. But before she could ask, Leona rattled on, "Howard, I do hope I can count on the use of some of your newer F150s to pull the floats."

"Floats?" Ruthie scoffed while Howard scratched his bald head. "Flatbed trailers draped with a few Christmas lights and some homemade poster boards ain't the kind of attractions that will bring people to town. Not when they can sit at home and dial up Netflix."

Leona clicked her pen. "Well, does anyone have a better idea?"

“What if we had a live nativity on one of the floats?” Etta May suggested. “If we play “Hark! The Herald Angels Sing” over the truck speakers that’s sure to put people in the mood to Christmas shop.”

“Sister,” Nola Gay said. “Do you remember the year the church tried having a live nativity in the town square?”

“Course I do.” Etta May peered over her glasses. “I was the angel everyone was harking.”

“Then you should remember how the stable goat ate all the hay in the manager then nearly choked on the plastic Jesus,” Ruthie said. “Nobody’s gonna have much of an appetite let for eatin’ at my diner if they have to watch Charlie drive up in his ambulance and perform the Heimy on a goat.”

While nods and commentary ensued about the year ambulance driver was called in to save the goat who ate the Christ child, Ruthie did the math. If this plan to bring folks to town really did work, how would she afford the supplies it would take to feed crowds? Her credit was already maxed with every vendor.

“You have a better suggestion, Ruthie?” Nola Gay snapped in defense of her sister.

“I’m just sayin—”

“All right.” Leona tapped her spoon against the side of her coffee mug until she had regained everyone’s attention. “Maybe it’s best if the nativity float does *not* have live animals.”

“Hold up, Leona,” Roxie said. “Etta May, may be on to something.”

“They’ll be plenty to clean up after that herd of horses Leona wants tramping down Main Street,” Howard said. “We don’t need goats.”

The used car salesman's grumbling spurred Roxie to dig in her spikey heels. "We've got to do something to put people in a shopping mood, or else there's really—"

"No point in having this ridiculous parade," Ruthie muttered, refusing to let her gaze encounter Angus in case he'd already figured out it took money to make money and since she had none, hitching her hopes to this plan was useless.

Leona charged on despite flailing support. "I'm proposing to run free ads for you in the *Messenger* that offer a discount to anyone who shops locally *after* the parade."

"But what if that doesn't get people into our businesses?" Angus asked.

"Your MeMaw could hand out free coffee and hot chocolate," Howard said.

Ruthie shook her head. "There you go again with me givin' things away for free."

"Howard has a point, Ruthie," Leona said. "You could give out a small free drink sample to entice people inside the diner for slivers of pie."

Ruthie crossed her arms over her ample chest. "There's no such thing as a sliver of pie in my diner."

"MeMaw," Angus said. "Mrs. L is just trying to help."

The bell above the door jangled. Everyone turned to see who the cold wind had blown in.

Wearing a cap pulled low, the stranger knocked water from his long, white beard. A tattered backpack hung from one shoulder. He scuffed the soles of his worn-out army boots on the mat. From the looks of him, life had been rough. Dollars to donuts he was one of the veterans living under the overpass at the edge of town. As a rule, Ruthie always did what she could for the folks who'd served. But if she kept feeding every down-on-his-luck soldier for free, she'd find herself pitching a tent next to them.

"Hey, mister," Ruthie pushed back from the table, intending to pour the stranger a cup of coffee and send him on his way. "Careful with them boots. I just mopped that floor."

"Sorry, ma'am." He adjusted the weight of his pack. "If you have a mop, I'd be happy to clean it up."

The small veterans' hospital on the military base outside of town attracted all sorts of ex-soldiers. The government couldn't do much more than put a bandage on their suffering. Nine times out of ten, they made their way to Ruthie's for a hot meal and a few moments relief from the cutting winds. She'd tried hiring a few of them. But in the end, they'd left her, some had even emptied her cash drawer on their way out. If this fella was expecting her to give him a job, the sooner she broke it to him straight, the sooner he could move on.

"Ain't got no work here," Ruthie said.

"I can do most anything." His voice had the gravely rasp of a chain smoker. "Was a fry cook in the army."

Ruthie pushed to her feet. "Any cookin' that gets done around here gets done by me."

Leona tugged Ruthie's sleeve. "It might not be a bad idea to hire someone to help you manage the parade crowd."

"The parade ain't for three weeks," Ruthie said, not willing to tell Leona that she had no idea how she was going to keep her doors open that long. "What will I do with him until then?"

"Train him," Leona said.

"For three weeks?"

Leona smiled sweetly. "I doubt three weeks is long enough to learn the complicated diner business." Although Leona had lost her position as the pastor's wife, she had not lost her drive for getting folks to do what she thought they ought.

"I got Angus," Ruthie countered.

"And he's proven himself quit the keeper," Leona agreed. "But it's a lot to expect the two of you to have this place shipshape for the onslaught of parade customers."

"Onslaught?" Ruthie's mind was counting how few cans she had on her shelves.

"The parade has always drawn a crowd," Leona said.

Ruthie huffed. "That's when we had a good Santa."

"Well, I, for one," Leona said, adding extra lift to her voice. "Am going to prepare for a fabulous day."

Ruthie cast her disagreement Leona's direction. "A little dust on the window ledges hasn't kept you and Mr. Levy from putting your feet under my tables." Ruthie had long ago given up the dream of owning the building outright so that she could expand the diner into a restaurant with white tablecloths and fold-out menus. "If people are expecting spit and polish, then they need to drive on to the Cracker Barrel in Amarillo."

"That's nearly a hundred miles away," Etta May said. "They could starve before they get there."

"They can either overlook a little dust and grease or they can drive on down the interstate."

"MeMaw," Angus pleaded. "What I think Mrs. L is trying to say is that we've only got one shot to put our best foot forward . . . for everyone." Angus nodded toward the man at the door like he was a full-bellied, flush-with-cash Santa instead of a man who could wrap his belt around his thin waist and empty wallet multiple times. "What would it hurt to freshen up the—"

"Now that you mention it," Howard stuck his big nose in the air and sniffed. "There *is* a disgusting smoky smell in here."

Ruthie reached across the table and grabbed Howard's coffee cup. "No more *free* coffee for you, Howard Davis."

"Fire!" Etta May shouted, pointing toward the wall of flames licking the plaster above the grill.

Ruthie's coffee mug shattered against the floor tiles as she scrambled toward the counter. "My grill's on fire!"

The bearded stranger dropped his backpack and shimmied out of his army jacket. Coat raised, he flew behind the counter with the speed of someone half his age. Ruthie legs seemed to move in slow motion as the man threw himself straight at the leaping flames. Pots and pans clattered to the floor.

"No!" Ruthie ripped off her apron and charged toward the smoke curling up from the man's singed jacket sleeves. By the time she reached the counter, the grease fire was out. "You fool." Ruthie's apron hung limp in her hand and her knees threatened to give out. "You could have been killed."

"This old building is a tinder box." The man straightened his smoldering jacket as he eyed the blackened grill. "Need to keep that grease trap cleaned."

"Don't tell me how to run my diner."

"Wouldn't dream of it." Charred bits of flapjacks fell from his jacket sleeves. "But cooks good as you are often far too busy doing the cooking to do grill maintenance."

"How do you know I'm a good cook?"

He nodded toward the gang gathering behind Ruthie. "You got customers, don't you?"

"It's none of your business what I got."

"I could clean that grease trap for fifteen bucks and one of those blue-plate chicken-liver dinner specials."

Ruthie planted her hands on her hips. "I'll clean my own trap—"

"MeMaw, look at his hands." Angus pointed at the man.

The old man glanced at his reddened palms then quickly hid them behind his back. "Ain't nothing."

"Quick," Leona said. "Get his hands into some cold water." She pushed past Ruthie and flipped on the sink faucet. "David, call Charlie and tell him we have a burn emergency."

"This old fool don't need an ambulance," Ruthie said, regretting being forced to allow her liability insurance to lapse. What would she do if he sued? She didn't even have enough cash saved up for this month's lease payment, let alone the three back payments she owed. No telling how much Charlie would charge her to flip on his flashing lights and drive this fool to the hospital.

"Ambulance?" The man swayed as he wiggled into his blackened coat. "I'm not going back to that hospital."

"Back?" Ruthie asked. "You sick?"

The stranger shook his head and hoisted the frayed pack over his shoulder. "Strong as an ox."

His coat hung from his bony shoulders and his cheeks were sunken hollows his beard could not hide.

"Can't tolerate liars." Ruthie snapped her apron and fumbled to tie the strings behind her back. "You're either sick or drunk."

The vagrant buttoned his coat. "If you don't have any work here, I'll be moving on."

"Wait," Angus said. "Charlie has lots of creams and bandages on his rig." He moved toward the old man, his voice lowered like he was trying to talk a feral cat out from behind the trash bin in the alley. "Charlie can probably treat your burns right here."

Beneath the weathered bill of his army cap, cloudy eyes flicked from Angus to Ruthie. "I'll wait for Charlie." The man held up his redden palms. "But only if you'll let me clean the grease trap to pay for his services."

"You saved our diner." Angus cut a glance at Ruthie. "Taking care of your medical tab is the least we can do. Right, MeMaw?"

"Well, I reckon—" Ruthie stuttered before she was cut off by Etta May.

"He needs a new coat too," Etta May said.

"And new boots," Nola Gay added.

"Y'all are sure generous with *my* money." Ruthie checked the knobs on the grill. "Angus, get this fool a cup of coffee *and* a sausage biscuit." She eyed the thin man eyeing her. "To go."

"MeMaw, it's freezing outside," Angus said. "He needs something that will stick to his ribs."

"I'll pay for his breakfast, Ruthie." Leona retrieved her purse from the table, then took out of her wallet. "And I'll pick up the tab on this odd job he wants to do for you."

Ruthie shook her head. "I don't need charity." At least not yet.

"This isn't charity." Leona fished two one-hundred-dollar bills from her wallet. She held them out and Howard's eyes about popped from his head.

Everyone knew Leona had come into a sizeable sum of money after her husband passed, but until this morning when the council found out she'd bought out Ivan, rarely had anyone witnessed her charitable deeds. She preferred keeping the financial contributions she made to college scholarships and new wings for the hospital anonymous.

Leona pushed the money into Ruthie's hand. "This is neighbor helping neighbor."

Ruthie pushed the money away. "I pay my own help."

A pleased smile lit Leona's pretty face. "Does that mean you'll employ this good man until after the Christmas parade?"

"Just because he flung his coat over a grill fire that don't make him a *good* man. He's obviously lying about his health. He could rob me blind then swear he didn't."

Leona patted Ruthie's arm. "After Charlie assesses his burns, I'll ask my Maddie if she has time to check him over at the hospital's outpatient clinic." Leona was always quick to toot the horn of her daughter, and well she should be. The sour-faced pastor's daughter had grown into a beautiful, brilliant, and charitable woman. She could have practiced medicine anywhere, but she'd chosen to come back to Mt. Hope to raise her children after she and her husband finished their missionary stint in Central America.

"If this old goat won't go to the hospital, what makes you think he'll see a doctor?" Ruthie felt her own blood pressure rising. If she didn't calm down, she'd find herself getting carried off in Charlie's ambulance.

"David can take him to see Maddie, then drop by the church's benevolence closet." Leona was not going to let this drop. "Once this brave man has had medical attention, a warm coat, and some new boots, he won't need to steal anything of yours, Ruthie."

The old soldier shook his head. "I don't deserve no benevolence."

"None of us do." David rubbed his chin the same way his daddy used to right before he offered a solution. "Tell you what sir, I have a few odd jobs at the church that need doing. I can pay you enough that you can spend a couple of nights at the Double D Motel."

The stranger stuck out his hand. "Sounds fair." He and David shook, and the deal was made before Ruthie could lodge her disapproval.

Etta May dug around in her big purse. "We'll donate several jars of pickles for him to snack on." She pulled out a Mason jar filled with green spears then thrust it at the old man. "If we fattened you up, I swear you'd look just like Santa. Don't you agree, Ruthie?"

"He looks more like a bag of trouble than a Santa Claus." Ruthie had fed hundreds of homeless veterans over the years. Not once had she felt threatened. This old man looked at her like she was a locked-up cash register. "I don't need no man's help. Especially one I don't know."

"MeMaw, please," Angus said.

Her reluctance to accept assistance from the council had put the hurt in her grandson's eyes and, heaven help her, hurt was something she swore she would never again inflict on a child of hers. Truth was the only thing she had left in this diner worth taking was her grandson's love.

"All right," Ruthie sighed. "But I'm counting on you to keep an eye on the cash register, you hear me, Angus?"

Her grandson hugged her. "Yes, ma'am." He turned and whispered to her new employee. "MeMaw's bark is worse than her bite."

The stranger's grin revealed a few random teeth. "Don't count on that, boy." He removed his hat. His hair had thinned, but without the shadow across his face, Ruthie's heart stopped. She would have known those bedroom eyes anywhere. "I'm grateful to you, Ruthie."

"Earl Dean Crouch." Ruthie whipped around, grabbed a cast iron skillet from the rack above the grill, then hurled it straight at the head of the man she'd sworn she never wanted see again.

Earl ducked.

The frying pan sailed through the front window, shattering the cup and saucer she'd painted on the large pane the day she and Earl had signed the lease on this place. Shards of glass rained down on Leona and Saul Levy's favorite booth.

"Now, Ruthie," Earl raised his palms and inched toward her. "I can—"

"Stand back." She snatched a bigger skillet from the rack and held it like a club. "How dare you turn up after all these years." Anger thrummed through her body. "You ever show your cowardly face in my diner again, Charlie will be carrying you out of here in a body bag."

CHAPTER SEVEN

Leona

Outside the diner, Ivan and Howard wrestled a piece of plywood over the gaping hole in the window. Inside, Roxie ignored Leona's whispered attempts to keep her from overexerting herself.

"I know what you're up to, Leona," Roxie said, glancing around to make sure no one was listening. "And while I appreciate your concern and would expect nothing less, I'm not completely broke and I'm not dead yet." Roxie picked up the dustpan. "I need you to believe God is going to help me beat this."

"I do believe that," Leona whispered. "I also believe God's expects us to do our part. Keeping Mt. Hope alive for years to come helps everyone."

"And saving Mt. Hope is your sole purpose in resurrecting the Christmas parade?"

Leona had never been able to be anything but truthful with Roxie. "You saved my life when you insisted I tackle my grief and fears by focusing on something productive."

"Is that why you bought the *Messenger*?"

"Maybe."

"Then why didn't you tell me you'd bought Ivan out?"

"I was going to call you after I finished my hospital rounds, but . . ." Leona couldn't bring herself to add her fear for Roxie's health to Roxie's worries.

Roxie blinked back tears then patted Leona's arm. "You're a good friend, Leona."

"Takes one to know one."

Roxie smiled, her first true and hopeful smile since her diagnosis. "Count me in on this plan of yours."

"Only if you count me in on any plan the doctors have for you."

"Fine," Roxie agreed. "But only if we keep the details to ourselves."

"Roxie, people want to help."

"I just need some time to process this, okay?"

Leona looked at her friend's lifted chin and the small flicker of fire in her eyes. This was Roxie's battle to fight and her story to write. Not hers. She couldn't heal Roxie's cancer, but she could be available whenever Roxie was ready to accept help. And she could pray.

Leona swallowed the lump in her throat. "Deal."

Roxie hugged her then turned to help Etta May and Nola Gay scoop up stray glass shards.

Across the diner, Ruthie sobbed into the shoulder of Angus's tweed sport coat. Leona hoped wearing J.D.'s old clothes would help Angus summon the words of comfort his grandmother needed because everyone deserved to be comforted with reassurances like Roxie had just given her.

"I can't believe we didn't recognize Earl Dean." Etta May emptied the dustpan into the trash bag Nola Gay held open. "Sister and I never forget a face."

"Ruthie didn't even recognize him," Nola Gay said. "And she was married to the man for nearly a year before he skedaddled for parts unknown." Nola Gay shook the bag and broken glass tinkled to the bottom. "You can look at him now and see that life on the run hasn't been good to him."

Whatever had happened between Ruthie and Earl Dean had happened long before Leona and her family moved to Mt. Hope.

Leona slid a chair a few inches in search of more broken glass. "Why did Ruthie's husband run?"

"If Ruthie knows, she's never said." Nola Gay plopped down on a chair opposite the booth. "But there've been plenty of speculation and rumors slung around over the years."

"Let's just stick to the truth, okay?" Roxie relieved Etta May of the whisk broom and Nola Gay of the trash bag. "You girls go on home before the weather gets worse," Roxie said. "Leona and I can finish up here."

Etta May peered around Leona's shoulder for one last peek at Ruthie. "Charlie says she's in shock."

"Our Ruthie's a strong woman." Leona gently turned Etta May toward the door. "She just needs a little time to process how she's going to forgive and forget."

"The man left her to raise their daughter alone," Etta May said, craning her neck for one last look. "You remember the toll little Ruby's wandering ways took on Ruthie, don't you Leona?"

"It was a sad time for sure," Leona agreed.

Nola Gay handed Etta May her purse then heaved herself out of the chair. "Leona, even you would have a hard time forgiving that man."

Etta May hefted Nola Gay's purse strap over her own shoulder. "And you're a saint."

"I'm no such thing. None of us are." Leona snagged Etta May's arm. "I can count on you two to keep this to yourselves, right?"

"Just because we run the prayer chain"—Nola Gay said— "that don't make us gossips."

Leona hoped Roxie wouldn't catch wind of the alert the twins had sent to David about her diagnosis. "Not one word of this to the prayer chain, you hear me?"

Etta May crossed her heart then pointed that very same index finger toward the sooty, tin-tiled ceiling. "Not even to the Big Guy upstairs?"

"You won't be telling God anything he doesn't already know," Leona reminded her. "But reminding him of how much our Ruthie needs some comfort right now surely can't hurt." She kissed their powdered cheeks. "The sleet's picked up. Be careful, ladies. The sidewalk might be slick."

Leona and Roxie worked in silence, each wrapped in their own thoughts of the future. Finally, when the last tiny broken piece of glass had been removed, Leona asked, "Roxie, do you know what happened between Ruthie and Earl?"

Roxie leaned on the handle of the big push broom. "A few weeks after I opened my parts store, Ruthie crossed the street to welcome me to Main Street. She found me sitting among boxes of unsold inventory and crying my eyes out. I told her I'd bitten off more than I could chew trying to be a wife and mother while starting a new business. Ruthie told me her story, but I'll not shame her by sharing the private details."

"Forgive me for asking."

"I owe Ruthie. It was her idea that I add tractor parts," Roxie said. "She may be a little gruff, but she's always been a good business neighbor. Beneath that elephant hide exterior is a surprisingly generous heart."

"She's been good to me."

"Before or after you two worked out where you could and could not park."

Leona and Roxie shared a laugh about those early days of Leona struggling to find her footing in the working world. Leona took the broom from Roxie. "You go on. Get your store's doors open. I'll see to Ruthie."

"No rush. It's not like folks are lined up these days." Roxie wiggled into her coat. "I saw Ivan snapping pictures. Is he staying on at the paper for a bit?"

"Says he's leaving after Thanksgiving."

"I'm not trying to tell you how to run your business . . ."

"But?"

"But, as the new owner of the *Messenger*, don't you think it would be better if you didn't run anything in the paper about the grill fire?"

"It's eyewitness news."

Roxie gave Leona's arm a supportive squeeze. "Bad news might sell papers, but Ruthie's right. If word gets out that there's a possibility of getting trapped in one of these old buildings, we might as well cancel any hope of attracting the customers we need to keep our doors open."

"Which is the whole point of the parade," Leona sighed in agreement. "Think we can keep Ruthie onboard?"

Roxie smiled. "The last thing Ruthie wants is for her ex-husband to see her give up."

"Nobody's giving up on my watch, right?"

"Hell's bells, Leona." Roxie flipped her glorious red hair over her coat collar. "We wouldn't dare."

"Then you'll let Maddie set up your treatment ASAP?"

"I'll think about it."

Leona watched Roxie cross the street. "Please, Lord," she whispered. "I'm not ready to lose my friend."

Leona blew out a sigh of frustration at her lack of control over this situation. Then she slowly made her way to the pantry to stow the broom. The shelves were nearly empty. She hefted the heavy trash bag and lugged it to the alley bin. Was Ruthie's low food stores the reason for her reluctance to get behind the parade plans? Only one way to find out.

Leona cleaned up the water her boots had tracked across the black and white tiles, then filled two ceramic mugs with the last of Ruthie's stout coffee.

She placed one cup in front of Ruthie and one in front of Angus. "Drink up, you two."

Angus removed his tight hold on his grandmother's shoulder and wrapped his shaky hands around the steaming mug. "I have a grandfather."

Leona gave him the reassuring smile his bewildered expression seemed to need. "So it would appear."

Ruthie's head snapped up. "That old man may have fathered this boy's mother, but he has never been a parent to anyone related to my Angus."

"Now, Ruthie—"

Griddle-hot heat leapt from the old woman's red-rimmed eyes. "I've got a broad back. Turned every disappointment and hardship that man dealt me into a roof over my family's head. But I can't bear to watch my grandson get his hopes up."

Leona pulled out a chair. "Ruthie, I'm sorry you've had such a shock."

Ruthie shook her head. "I don't know why I'm surprised that he'd turn up now."

"What makes you say that?"

"Did you see how he swayed?"

"He was probably very nervous."

"He's probably dying, Leona, and he's come back expecting me to take care of him."

Angus stiffened. "If you thought he was sick, MeMaw, why'd you send him out in this weather?"

"Angus," Ruthie tried to soften the edge to her voice, but it was still razor sharp. "I know you love to take in every stray pup that comes along. But taking in that old cur is a good way to get bit."

"But MeMaw—"

"Remember Ollie?" Ruthie interrupted. "I hired that vagrant friend of yours as a fry cook to make *you* happy. Then Ollie went and put marijuana in the brownies for the church's Christmas Eve reception." Ruthie was a dog with a bone when it came to shaking out the worst from a mistake. "You'd both still be in jail if Leona's new husband hadn't helped me scrape together enough bail money."

"Ollie sobered up." Leona hadn't eaten another brownie of any kind. Her love of chocolate had been ruined that embarrassing night. But if she hadn't been high, Saul Levy would never have had to put her to bed. When she awoke, still fully dressed, that's when she discovered she'd fallen in love with a true gentleman. She owed Ollie. She owed Ruthie a chance to find the same peace and happiness she'd found. "And he paid off his debt by working for you for months."

"And just when I started to trust him," Ruthie countered. "He went to Minnesota to live with his daughter." Ruthie crossed her arms over her ample bosom. "That's the thanks you get when you put yourself out there."

"Ollie had a chance to make amends to his family." Angus was doing his best to keep his emotions in check, but his desperation was a pot on the verge of boiling over. "MeMaw, you were the one who bought his bus ticket so he could go," he paused, as if he knew what he must say next might hurt her. "What if PePaw came back to make amends?"

"PePaw?" Ruthie snorted. "Where on earth did you come up with a name like PePaw?"

He smiled broadly. "Rhymes with MeMaw." Short of dropping to his knees and begging, Angus was doing his best to soften her up. "Surely you'd want me to know the only grandfather I've got." He pushed back from the table, a hunger in his eyes unlike anything Leona had ever seen. "I'm going after him."

Ruthie bowed up. "You walk out that door, and you can just keep on going."

Angus grinned, secure in the fact that the same grandmother who'd bailed him out of jail after the pot brownie incident wouldn't let him go hungry for anything...even chasing after a relationship with the man who'd abandoned them. "I'll be back in time to help with the lunch crowd. I promise, MeMaw."

"That's what Earl Dean said forty years ago," Ruthie shouted after him.

"I'm not Earl Dean, I just want to know him." The slamming of the diner door nearly jostled the bell off its bracket.

Leona and Ruthie sat in silence. Unsure what to say next.

"Crowd?" Ruthie sighed, waving a weary hand over the empty diner. "Does it look like I need Earl Dean's help around here, Leona?"

Leona wanted to reach for the woman, to scoop her into her arms and tell her everything would be all right. But she knew from her own experience with a painful emotional shock that a person needed supportive friends, not promises they may or not be able to deliver.

"Ruthie, life has made you into a strong woman."

"Don't go to preachin', Leona. That pastor boy of yours is the only Harper who can hold my attention through a sermon."

Maybe she should have let Roxie be the one to try to talk sense into Ruthie. "I'm just trying to say that I've never seen you be anything but fair."

"Earl Dean's the one who left." She jabbed her pointer finger at the door. "Not me."

Leona understood the anger that came with the unexpected departure of a loved one. She'd still be angry at J.D. if she'd not made a conscious effort to forgive him for dying without asking her permission. "I'd give anything for the opportunity to ask J.D. why he didn't take better care of himself, especially when he noticed he was short-winded."

Ruthie leaned forward. "You want me to ask Earl Dean why he left?"

"Don't you want to know?" Leona failed to keep the surprise out of her voice.

"I know."

"You do?"

"I do."

"Then why did he go?"

Silence followed that question, but Leona thought helping Ruthie voice the answer she'd believed all these years would give her insight into how to help Ruthie navigate this new hurt. "Why do believe Earl Dean left, Ruthie?"

"I wasn't enough." Ruthie lifted her chin. "And I won't ever be."

Chapter Eight

Leona

Leona's hospital cafeteria coffee had gone cold thirty minutes ago. She checked her phone for a message. Still no explanation from her daughter as to why Maddie had agreed to meet her and was now making her wait.

She knew Maddie's life had become extremely busy since she and Parker returned from the mission field. Not only was her daughter's little family in the process of acclimating to life back in the States, they were also trying to raise two small children while restoring Parker's ranch to a full operational status and getting Maddie's new medical practice set up. That's why Leona rarely intruded. But her question was important. And she could tell from the serious tone of Maddie's voice when she'd phoned that Maddie was taking Roxie's situation hard as well.

"Sorry you had to wait, Momma," Maddie said as she slid into the dining chair opposite Leona. "Had an unexpected burn patient. David said something about a little grill fire at the Koffee Kup. You there when it happened?" Her daughter's face was flushed from hurrying, and she had dark circles under her eyes from the sleepless nights her toddler was still dishing up, but beneath the stress of it all, Maddie was happy. And seeing her daughter so happy after so many years of worrying she might not ever be made Leona happy and grateful to God.

Leona nodded. "The man you treated is Ruthie's ex-husband."

"Whoa," Maddie said. "There's a story here you're not telling me."

"There's a story Ruthie's not telling," Leona agreed. "But I've got bigger fish to fry right now." Leona reached across the table and squeezed Maddie's hand. "How's my girl?"

Maddie eyed her skeptically. "Running on fumes."

"You're in a season of life that feels like it will last forever but, in truth, it goes by in a flash."

"Isn't that true of all of our lives, Momma?"

Her daughter had grown into a beautiful and wise woman despite every mistake Leona had made while raising her. It was all Leona could do not to cry. "Yes, my love. Life is short." Leona pushed her coffee mug aside. "Which is why I want to know what you can tell me about Roxie."

"Momma, if you're here to gather medical intel on your best friend," Maddie said. "You know I won't break the HIPAA confidentiality rules."

"You've seen her chart though, right?"

"Dr. Boyer asked me for a second opinion."

"All I'm asking is your best-case scenario generalities."

Maddie studied her for a long moment, then finally said, "Encourage Aunt Roxie to get on this ASAP, okay?"

Leona flinched at the note of urgency Maddie had allowed to raise her voice. "Roxie's stubborn," Leona said. "She watched her mother suffer through chemo. I'm not sure she'll agree to go through those treatments."

"Has her doctor confirmed she's going to need chemo?"

"Well, no. Not that I know of," Leona admitted. "But I know her, and once she's had time to consider her options, I want to make sure she's not going to mess around with this."

"Momma." Maddie waved both hands in surrender. "Aunt Roxie is loud, brave, and beautiful. But she's no match for you when it comes to getting people to do what they've always said they would never do."

Chapter Nine

Ruthie

Ruthie tossed her sponge in the bucket of scummy water, planted her hands near the ache in her lower back and surveyed the damage to her diner. Soot blackened the walls above the stainless-steel panel behind her old, gas-fueled flattop. The loss could have been worse. Would have been worse if Earl Dean hadn't risked his life and thrown himself on the flames.

Nope.

She refused to give that sorry scoundrel an ounce of credit for thinking about someone besides himself for a change. If he was so good at saving things, why hadn't he tried to save their marriage years ago? How many fires had she put out while he was gone? Five? Ten? Fifteen? Too many to count, especially if she threw in all the troublesome fires Ruby had stirred up. While she was busy doing what simply had to be done, Earl Dean was out galivanting around the country and living his life without a care.

Ruthie lumbered to the storage closet, muttering curses on the coward who'd dared to burst in after all these years and pretend to be her hero.

The stepladder was wedged in behind the last few cans of gravy and banana pudding. Before the arches in her feet fell, everything she served in her diner was made from scratch. Nowadays, the pain in her flat feet shot all the way up her legs and squeezed the get-up-and-go from her belly. It was all she could do to keep up with the occasional pie order and fry burgers for her only two lunch regulars: Leona and Saul Levy.

Maybe it would have been better if Earl Dean had let this place burn to the ground. If she hadn't allowed her renter's insurance to lapse at least she'd have gotten a little bit of cash to weather her old age.

With a heave, she hoisted the wooden stepladder off its hook and dragged it to the grill. Angus would throw a wall-eyed fit if he caught her climbing this rickety old thing while toting a bucket of soapy water. Her grandson had had a hard life. Deserted by his father. Left alone to tend to his sick mother. Orphaned at sixteen. When he'd finally made his way to her, she'd wanted to spare him more hurt. She would not make the skeletons in her closet his problem.

Ruthie dropped the bucket handle into the crook of her arm and slowly began to climb the ladder.

Earl Dean's unexpected reappearance had unearthed all sorts of feelings, and not just for her. Angus might eventually get over his disappointment of her withholding information about his grandfather. But he wouldn't give up on having the family he'd always wanted. She wouldn't be the least bit surprised if Angus insisted she give Earl Dean a second chance.

"Second chance, my foot." Ruthie plunged her rag into the dirty water and swiped at the sooty wall. "Second chance to clean out my cash register is more like it."

It kinked her gut to ponder Earl Dean's sudden return. Did he want something? Did he know she'd never filed for divorce? Did he know that technically he still owned half interest in the diner? If that old fool thought putting out a little grease fire meant she'd split the proceeds of the sale of all the diner contents, he was missing more than a few teeth in his head.

She'd spent nearly forty years cleaning up the mess Earl Dean's sudden disappearance had made of her life. She wasn't about to let his sudden reappearance mess up Angus.

Ruthie studied the smoke trail that snaked all the way up the wall from the grill to the pressed-tin ceiling. This clean-up job required fortification. She slid the bucket handle into the crook of her arm, then climbed down from the ladder, careful not to let the gray water slosh onto the floor. She emptied the bucket contents into the sink, then poured herself another cup of coffee. Stirring in two sugar packets, her thoughts spun back to the last time Earl Dean came home.

He'd been a soldier stationed overseas for seven months. Proudly serving his country on the front lines. By the time his tour was up, she was eight months pregnant and the size of a beached whale. She wanted him to think she was still beautiful, so on the day he'd been scheduled to arrive home, she spent extra time on her hair and makeup.

Dust swirled around the Greyhound when it pulled to a stop. Her heart was fizzy as the root beer floats she and Earl Dean used to share. She'd been running the diner on her own for months. Keeping things going until her handsome husband came home. What if he didn't like the stainless-steel backsplash she'd added behind the grill? Earl Dean always said people went to diners for the food, not the ambiance, so she'd worked extra hard on her cooking. She'd even added blue-plate specials and perfected her grandmother's homemade pie recipes.

She'd done all these things for them.

For their future, and the future of their baby.

One by one, soldiers descended the bus steps. Square-shouldered boys had gone off to war. Slump-shouldered and bleary-eyed men returned. Ruthie waited anxiously, rising on her tiptoes as she searched for Earl Dean. But when the trickle of men leaving the bus dried up, there was no Private Crouch among them. Clutching her baby bump, Ruthie craned her neck. Where was her husband? Finally, when no more men appeared at the bus door, she made her way through the dispersing crowd. She braced herself against the folding bus door and asked the driver if he'd seen a tall, freckle-faced redhead.

He reached for the door lever. "No, ma'am."

"Can you check the bus, please?"

The beefy man looked at her big belly. With a sigh, he released the door lever, then threw the gearshift into park. "You might be better off if he ain't here, lady."

The driver stomped to the back of the bus. Standing with her hand shielding her eyes from the sun, Ruthie watched as the driver stopped at the back of the bus then bent down and fished someone out from under the seat. She could tell the fellow the driver had rousted was thinner than how she remembered Earl Dean, but the sound of his agitated voice was unmistakable. What didn't sound like Earl Dean was his adamant denial that Mt. Hope was his stop.

The driver shoved the reluctant soldier out the door. Ruthie bent far as her stomach would allow to help the man sprawled facedown at her feet.

"Earl Dean?" He'd lost so much weight he was easy for her to get upright. "Earl Dean, you sick?"

His hand flew to protect his eyes from the sun, or so she thought. But in truth, it seemed he didn't want her looking at him. "I'm sorry, Ruthie. I'm so sorry."

"What've you got to be sorry about?" She threw her arms around his twig-thin body. "You're home."

His hug had been disappointingly stiff, but not as disappointing as the fact that he didn't even mention her belly. He was tired, she'd told herself as she helped him to his feet. From what little she'd seen of the war on her black and white television, no wonder his time in the jungle had put that scared rabbit look in his eyes.

"You need a good meal." Her arm linked in his. Slowly, she walked him to the apartment she'd fixed up above the diner. He didn't say a word about the potted mums beside the door or the recently installed Koffee Kup sign blinking in the diner's window. She led him up the narrow stairs. "Earl Dean, you rest here on the sofa while I'll slip down to the grill and fix you a feast." She squatted despite the pain the effort brought to her knees and untied his boots. "Burger and fries sound good?"

He gave her a tired nod. Fifteen minutes later, she set the steaming plate before him, but he never took a bite. Just sat on the sofa, smoking one cigarette after another, his hands shaking like he was freezing to death in the stifling Texas heat.

As the days wore on, Ruthie wore down.

But she was determined to help her husband find his way back to her. "You start cooking again, Earl Dean, and you'll start to feel like your old self." She coaxed him downstairs, led him to the grill, cinched his chef's apron around his thin middle, and handed him his favorite spatula. "Go on, now. Show me some of that fancy grub you learned to make while you were cooking for all those soldier boys."

Earl Dean tried several times to make hash, but he was jumpy as a strip of bacon on a hot griddle. No matter how careful she was to keep things quiet, every time she set a pot lid or scrapped the grease drippings into the trap, he'd startle at the noise, rip off his apron, and rush out the back door of the diner.

At first, he just paced the alley and smoked. But after a few days, he refused to come back inside until he'd smoked a whole pack and ground the butts into the cobblestones with his army boots. Eventually, it got to where he didn't stop to do his smoking in the alley. He'd fly out the back door of the diner, then disappear to heaven knows where, only to come back hours later out of cigarettes and inconsolably agitated.

Then one day, she accidentally dropped a plate. The shattering noise startled Earl Dean so bad he grabbed his hat, shot out the back screen door, and never came back.

The mug in Ruthie's hand grew heavy at the memory of that heart-splintering day. She set her coffee on the counter, refilled her cleaning bucket with hot soapy water, then climbed the ladder. As she began to scrub, suds cut tear streaks through the soot.

"MeMaw!" The alarm in Angus's voice as he burst through the diner's front door rattled the soda glasses and gave Ruthie a start. "What do you think you're doing?"

Ruthie wheeled. The unfortunate overreaction to Angus's scolding left her with only one leg securely planted on the ladder's top rung. She wobbled, but then somehow miraculously managed to turn and plant her flailing foot back on the thin step with a stomp.

"What does he think he's doing here?" she jerked a nod toward the man who'd trailed in after Angus. "Earl Dean, I told you to let my grandson be."

Earl Dean's eyes cut from Angus to Ruthie. "*He* came after me."

Was he implying *she* should have charged after him? Tried harder to find him?

If he only knew how much tire rubber she'd wasted scouring the back roads of Texas looking for him. She'd probably still be checking cardboard tents built under the overpasses if little Ruby hadn't insisted on being born two days after he cut out on them. That girl of hers always did have the worst timing. After Ruby was born, Ruthie spent her days trying to keep a roof over their heads and her nights trying to soothe a crying baby. There were no spare minutes left to look for a man who'd gone AWOL from his responsibilities.

"MeMaw, please climb down," Angus inched forward slowly, wiggling the fingers on his outstretched hand. "PePaw and I can wash the walls."

"That's right." Earl Dean took a step forward. "Let us help."

"I don't need help! From either of you."

"MeMaw—"

"Angus," she growled, not trying to reel in her anger. "I know you think I just look for ways to pop holes in your grandiose ideas, but you can't save every down-and-out soul you encounter."

"You saved me, MeMaw."

"That's different," Ruthie said. "You're family."

Angus hooked a thumb toward Earl Dean. "He's family."

Earl Dean removed his hat and tucked it under his arm. From her perch, she could see his bare scalp. A thin snowy fringe encircled the place where thick red curls had once tumbled across his forehead. He lifted his face, an oval that matched the same upturned nose sprinkled with the same freckles as Angus. Earl Dean's ruddy cheeks had the dark age spots of a man who'd spent far too many years out in the elements, but she was certain that if she gave him the shave he needed, she'd find the same square chin of her grandson. The only difference between the two men trying to sweettalk her off the ledge was that Earl Dean's cloudy blue eyes carried the same wanderlust she'd seen the first day they met—a restlessness she'd foolishly thought she could tame.

Ruthie aimed her sponge at Earl Dean. "Nobody tried harder to save you than I did, Earl Dean Crouch." Water dripped on the black and white floor tiles. "You left without so much as a note on a napkin." Her voice rose another notch. "You have no idea of the pain and suffering I went through raising our daughter alone while trying to keep a roof over our heads and—"

"MeMaw, you always say a pancake has two sides," Angus pled. "Can't we at least hear his side?"

"Tell him the truth, Earl Dean. Tell him who you really are."

Shame washed over Earl Dean's weathered face. "Ruthie, I don't deserve anything for the—"

"No." Ruthie stomped her foot. "You don't get to come waltzing in with some sob story and expect me to welcome you back with open arms." She stomped with her full weight.

Crack.

The ladder rung beneath her feet splintered.

The ladder swayed.

“MeMaw!” Angus knocked chairs out of his way. “Hang on.”

Ruthie grabbed for the plate rack but before she could get a good hold, the ladder rung ripped away. “Earl—”

***

Ruthie woke to the pungent odor of Pine Sol. It took a moment for the bright room to come into focus. Stark white walls. Pristine white ceiling tiles. Not a smudge of soot. When had she finished her cleaning job?

“Ruthie?” Leona reached over the bed rail and patted her hand. “Ruthie, do you remember what happened?”

Images of Angus and Earl Dean coming through her diner door, arm in arm like long lost friends, rotated around and around in her hazy view. Earl Dean had taken from her every dream of building a life with the man she loved. She was not going to let that no-good drifter take Angus.

Anger strong enough to knock Earl Dean into the next county surged through her. She tried to sit up. But her limbs wouldn’t cooperate. She blinked until the gritty image of Earl Dean stealing Angus away from her receded and the concern on Leona’s face sharpened.

Leona asked her question again, this time louder as if Ruthie had somehow lost her hearing when she lost her temper. If she’d learned anything about Leona, it was that the woman was persistent. Leona’s need to get to the bottom of things made her a good reporter, but a nosy friend. Sooner or later, she would expect Ruthie to answer.

Until she had a coherent response, she'd stall.

Ruthie let her gaze trace the pain radiating from her throbbing head to her aching foot.

A thick white cast wrapped her right leg from the tip of her unpainted toenails to just below the bend in her knee. A matching cast held her aching wrist in place.

"I remember ..." the words caught in Ruthie's dry throat.

Leona leaned in closer. "What do you remember, Ruthie?"

"I remember that Earl Dean Crouch broke my heart." She glanced at her matching casts. "Now that old coward has done gone and broke my limbs."

Chapter Ten

Leona

Leona fussed around Roxie's recliner. Plumping the pillows behind her friend's head, under her feet, and under the arm on the side where she'd had breast surgery.

"I thought you were sitting with Ruthie."

"She's in rehab." Leona put a homemade protein drink within Roxie's easy reach. "Besides she told me I needed to be with you."

"She probably just needed a break from your mothering."

"Is that why you're bucking to get back to work?" Leona didn't let Roxie answer. "I think you should follow Dr. Boyer's orders and take a few more days before you go full bore."

"It was just a little lumpectomy, Leona." Roxie let her head sink back into the neck pillow. "Even Maddie said it was good news that the surgeon felt certain he'd gotten it all."

"But the surgeon said you could face further treatments once the lab results come back on the tumor."

"Then we'll cross that bridge when we come to it."

"What would it hurt to rest for another day or two? It's not like—"

"Business is booming on Main Street?"

"Well, not yet, but I'm just getting started."

"Hell's bells, Leona. You've practically spoon fed me since I came home. You can't sit around here changing the TV channels for me if you're going to pull off this business-saving Christmas parade of yours."

"Lucky for you, and all the businesses on Main Street," Leona smiled proudly. "I've learned to multi-task." She pointed at her laptop. "While you've been sleeping, I've been working."

"Oh, yeah?"

Leona pulled a chair close to Roxie's recliner and flipped open her laptop. "I've got a to-do spreadsheet. See?"

"Of course, you do."

Leona pointed at the lines on the screen. "My first goal is to launch our Christmas parade campaign with a local essay contest."

"Essays?"

"You know, short stories about past Christmas parades, what Christmas means to me, etc."

"Leona, I may be in the tractor parts business, but I know what essays are," Roxie saw Leona stiffen and backed up her disapproval. "I'm just wondering how you plan to generate participation."

"I've already convinced the school principals to enlist their teachers in encouraging the children to participate," Leona hurried on. "There'll be cash prizes for each age group, and I'll publish the winner's pictures in the paper."

"Everyone loves to see their kid's picture in the paper."

"Exactly." Leona scrolled to the next screen. "Angus has agreed to put his business-slash-marketing degree to work."

"How so?"

"I've hired him to slip next door to work for me during the slow times at the diner. He's rebranding Mt. Hope by highlighting local attractions like the annual Christmas parade. And here's the best part, Angus and Modyne are taking the paper digital with a snazzy new website. It should be up and running in the next twenty-four hours."

"Wow, I'm impressed you managed to convince Ruthie and Modyne to jump on board with this."

"Well, technically, Angus and I have decided not to worry Ruthie with the details of his side hustle. As for Modyne, she couldn't resist the idea once I pointed out that she's an absolute whiz on the computer," Leona said. "And that's not all," Leona went on. "I've asked Parker to write a weekly ranch report. His article can include anything from highlighting the weather forecast to showcasing the Story sisters' stem rot."

"Complete with pictures, I'm assuming."

"Complete with Ivan's stunning pictures," Leona beamed.

"So, I take it that Ivan has agreed to stay on and get behind your grand plans?"

"Well, technically I've not officially asked him, but . . ."

"But how could he resist your charms, right?"

"Ivan is lost right now. He needs us."

"Ivan's a lucky man to have you in his corner." Roxie reached for her hand. "Technically, we all are. Now, tell me the rest."

Leona swallowed hard. "We're setting up targeted advertising campaigns that hit Facebook, Instagram, TikTok, and anything else Angus believes might have an audience." She grabbed a quick breath. "I'm also going to highlight the hospital with updates about our recent equipment acquisitions as well as our new specialty care providers. I plan to itemize our wide range of services and showcase our ability to provide first-rate healthcare for the entire region."

"Leona, this is brilliant." Roxie's face glowed with pride. "And you thought you hadn't acquired any skills after thirty years of planning ladies' teas armed with nothing more than a can of tuna."

"Sometimes you have to get down the road a bit before you can look back and see the goodness of God."

"Was that bit of wisdom for me or for you?"

"Both."

They sat in the silence of two friends soaking in the years of special moments God had given them. Leona prayed the Lord would grant them many more.

"Leona," Roxie said. "Think you've got room on that spreadsheet of yours for one more idea?"

"Always."

"It's going to take a little leg work, and a healthy shot of that convincing charm of yours."

"We're having a Christmas parade, aren't we?"

They both laughed.

Roxie leaned forward with a grimace. "You're sure you can convince Ivan to stick around until after the parade, right?"

"I can't tie him to his desk, but that's the agreement and Ivan has always been a man of his word."

"Good," Roxie said. "My idea has to be fully operational *before* Angus springs Ruthie out of rehab."

"If you're thinking what I'm think you're thinking," Leona smiled. "I'm already on it."

Chapter Eleven

Leona

"Ivan, the pics you got yesterday are amazing." Leona couldn't help smiling as she clicked through the images on her computer screen. "These are exactly what Roxie had in mind."

"And they're selling papers," Modyne said. "Subscriptions are up twenty-five percent just since Angus launched our first batch of Facebook ads."

"That's terrific news!" Leona said. "I'll ask David and Maddie for permission to upload the shot of my grandkids to all our sites ASAP. Angus, maybe you could build an ad with their pic in the meme."

Angus swiveled in the desk chair he'd shoved next to Modyne. "Listen to you, Mrs. L. You sound like you've been running an internet business for years."

"Old dogs can learn new tricks, kiddo."

Angus dropped his chin on his cupped hand. "Hope MeMaw agrees."

"Ruthie's tough, but she's also proven herself to be one sharp businesswoman," Leona said. "What's best for Mt. Hope is also what's best for her and what's best for her is what's best for you. Don't worry, Angus. She'll come around. You'll see." Leona looked up to find Ivan standing beside her desk, tears swimming in his eyes. "Ivan, what's wrong?"

"I . . ." he stammered. "Selling the paper to you was the right decision."

Her heart broke for the brokenness she saw in her friend. She'd been so busy trying to save the world, she hadn't even considered how the success it brought to the paper might make her friend feel. "Ivan, we're not doing anything here that you wouldn't have thought of."

He shook his head. "That's sweet, Leona, but you know that's not true." He handed her an envelope. "I'm returning your earnest money."

"Ivan, you need this money."

"Don't feel like I can take it since I'm breaking our agreement and leaving town early."

"Wait," Leona pushed back from her desk. "Ivan, please."

He picked up his camera bag. "Some old dogs are just too worn out to learn new tricks."

"Ivan, I don't need you to learn new tricks." She took him by the elbow and led him to his empty desk. "I need you to do what you do best."

"Run a newspaper into the ground?"

"Nobody captures the essence of a story with a camera lens like you do." She perched on the corner of his desk. "Listen to me, Ivan. I know what it feels like to be at loose ends after the loss of the love of your life. Some days it was all I could do to get out of bed. But I promise there is light at the end of the tunnel."

A tear slid down his cheek. “Leona, I’m just slowing you down.”

“I slowed you, and this newspaper, way down for more than a year, but you didn’t give up on me.”

“That was different.”

“I don’t see how, but I’m not going to argue semantics with you,” Leona said. “How about this? You stay on as my ace photographer. Help me rally this town with a visual portfolio that will give this Christmas parade the legs it needs to make a difference here. Make a difference for your family.”

“You know I don’t have any family.”

Leona took a breath. “The truth is, Ivan Tucker, we’re family in this town and family doesn’t bail on family. Do you know who taught me that?”

He shrugged. “Me?”

“Bingo.” She took his face in her hands. “Hear me, Ivan. You were the first person to give me a second chance. You taught me everything I know about the newspaper business. You gave me a shot at more than a career, you gave me a new purpose. And I’ll never forget what you did for me. Please stay.” She released his face, then sat back. Wading through grief was like wading through mud. It took effort. It hurt. It felt like drowning. She held out her hand. “Let me help you.”

“Okay, Leona,” Ivan heaved a heavy sigh and put his hand in hers. “I’ll get the shots for your interest stories, and I’ll even stay until the end of the parade.”

Leona swallowed the lump in her throat. “You won’t be sorry, Ivan.”

Chapter Twelve

Ruthie

"I told Angus to bring the truck and come for me." Ruthie sat with her arm propped on a lap pillow and her casted leg crammed in between Leona's passenger seat and the dashboard of her fancy car.

"Your grandson's busy at the diner."

"Doing what?"

Leona waved goodbye to the nurse who'd wheeled Ruthie to the rehab facility's pickup curb. "Getting ready for the parade. It's only a week away."

"I told that boy to close down the diner until I was on my feet again."

"Angus didn't want you to miss out on the business."

"One day of customers isn't going to be enough to keep my doors open." The confession felt good. A relief.

Leona nodded as if she'd known all along about the eviction notice. "The council's plan is already bringing business back to Main Street."

"What do you mean…already?"

"It's a Christmas miracle, Ruthie." Leona pressed on the gas. "People everywhere. Lots of them."

"Really?" Hope flickered for a second. Then Ruthie remembered her hospital bills. If she thought she was short on cash before, her foolish accident had sealed her inability to afford enough food for a decent snack let alone a crowd. "I don't think I'm up to parade day." Ruthie stared out the window, blinking away tears. "We'll just put a closed sign in the window."

"Maybe you should wait until you see what Angus has done before you do anything hasty."

Angus had all sorts of business plans, and they were all impressive. No denying that. And if she had the funds, she'd have given him free rein to help her get her diner business financially squared away when he came home from college. She knew her boy well enough to know that until he was certain she was taken care of, he'd never feel good about setting out on his own.

"Angus knows not to do anything to my diner without checking with me first."

"I've already said too much." Leona kept her eyes on the road. "I don't want to ruin his surprise."

Ruthie used to love surprises. Then Earl Dean gifted her with two of the biggest surprises of her life: his big exit hole in her heart, and then his recent re-entry hole.

Now that she'd had decades to reflect on how skittish her husband had been when he came back from the war, she shouldn't have been surprised when he left. Maybe if she could have found him some help, no matter how much it cost, things would have been different. But she was young and stupid, and besides, nobody talked about the post traumatic effects of war back then. Though she'd come to know so much more about the troubles soldiers faced when they returned from war, she still didn't know the best way to help him now.

"I don't like surprises," Ruthie muttered.

"Relax, Ruthie." Leona flipped her turn signal. "Everything's going to be just fine."

Traffic was so backed up on Main Street that they came to a stop. Parking slots on both sides of the street were filled for three blocks.

Ruthie leaned forward. "What in tarnation is going on at Roxie's?" Outside of Brewer Auto & Tractor Parts, Roxie wove in and out of the line of people stretched almost to the pharmacy. "I thought you said Roxie was recovering from surgery."

"She's doing better than expected."

"Must be if she's already giving away free tractor tune ups."

"Well, truth is . . ." Leona hemmed and hawed before she finally said, "She's hired a Santa."

"A Santa?" Small children darted between the clumps of chatting parents. "Why on earth would she do that? Kids don't buy tractor parts."

"No," Leona admitted. "But they have parents who do."

"Well, ain't she the clever one?" Ruthie craned her neck to get a better view of the crowd. "Who'd she find to play Santa?"

"The perfect candidate presented himself," Leona hedged. "Her come-meet Santa ads and pictures in the *Messenger* are already bringing folks in from several counties."

"I haven't seen any pictures."

"They're in our digital version." Leona nodded at the crowd and changed the subject. "Roxie told me she acquired her head for business from watching you."

Ruthie wouldn't argue that statement, so she let it go and repeated her question. "Who'd Roxie hire?"

"I think we're going to have to unload you at the diner's back door." Leona turned down the alley as easily as she avoided giving a straight answer. She pulled to a stop at the diner's loading ramp. "Yes, this will work. We can wheel you up and straight in."

The ice had long-since melted during Ruthie's seven-day stay in rehab, but in the shadow of the two-story building, the cobblestones were still slick.

"I'll call Angus and ask him to come help you get that heavy wheelchair out of the trunk." Ruthie pulled out her cell phone. "Don't want my chair getting away from you."

"I managed my mother's wheelchair for months after her tumble down the parsonage stairs, remember?" Leona patted her arm. "Sit tight."

A few minutes later, Leona had Ruthie unloaded and cradling the potted ivy and get-well card the city council had sent. Leona pushed Ruthie up the small cement ramp. Holding the screen door open with her backside, Leona managed to give the heavy metal door a shove. She wrestled the wheelchair over the threshold and into the small pantry. Familiar aromas drifted over Ruthie. Fried chicken livers. Fried pies. French fried potatoes.

"Angus," Ruthie called, unable to fight the tears. "Feels so good to be home with my boy."

"Hold on to that feeling." Leona spun the wheelchair around. "Angus," she called as they wheeled through the pantry. "She's here."

When Leona rolled Ruthie around the counter, the entire dining room erupted in applause and shouts of, "Surprise!"

The diner hadn't been this full of patrons in years. Kids swiveled on every counter stool. Parents packed every booth. Farmers and ranchers surrounded every single table. Several groups of out-of-towners Ruthie didn't recognize waited to be seated at the new welcome station.

Welcome station?

Despite all the clapping and cheering, Ruthie couldn't peel her gaze away from the preacher-like podium positioned just inside her front door.

"Is that J.D. Harper's old pulpit?" As Ruthie turned to Leona for an explanation, she caught sight of Angus. "What have you done, young man?"

"MeMaw!" A dusting of flour covered his freckles and new grease splatters covered her old chef's apron. He tucked a pencil above his ear and waved her favorite spatula. "Welcome back!"

"You've been busy."

His grin lit up his eyes. "Yes, ma'am." He turned and skillfully slid the spatula under two burgers and flipped both patties at the same time. "Couldn't handle the crowds without the help of Mrs. L and everyone on the council."

"The council?" Ruthie quickly surveyed the room again.

Nola Gay lifted a small jar of pickles from the basket draped over her arm in salute, then proudly set the jar before a man stuffing a fried chicken liver into his mouth. He tipped the brim of his cowboy hat and returned to his food.

Etta May turned from the milkshake machine, plopped a pickled crab apple on top of the exorbitant pile of whipped cream, smiled at Ruthie then sent the strange concoction sliding down the counter and into the arms of an excited little boy.

Howard Davis stood by the pulpit, tugging at his bow tie while asking the names of those waiting at the door and carefully writing them in a Bible-sized ledger.

"Smile, Ruthie." Ivan held up his camera, clicked, and the flash nearly blinded her. "Front-page interest story."

"Well..." Ruthie blinked and stammered. "I never."

"You must be hungry after a week of hospital food." Angus flipped a perfectly charred patty onto a lightly toasted bun. "This burger has your name on it, MeMaw."

Ruthie passed her potted plant to Leona and tried to get out of her chair. "I can't let y'all wait on me."

"You've waited on all of us for years." Leona pressed Ruthie back into her seat. "Today, you rest. Saul and I saved you a place at our booth." She handed Ruthie her potted plant, then wove her in and around the crowded tables with the skill of someone who'd been steering stubborn women toward different ways of looking at things all her life.

Saul stood like the gentleman that he was, took Ruthie by the elbow, and helped her ease onto the padded booth seat.

It wasn't until her backside failed to sink into one of the hollows created by the coffee klatch of old men who used to meet for breakfast in this booth every Wednesday, that Ruthie noticed the booth seats had been reupholstered. She searched her dining room for other changes. The walls had been painted a light sunny buttercup. And the broken windowpane (from the day she'd thrown her best scramble skillet at Earl) had been replaced.

"Who did all of this?" she asked Leona.

"Santa." Leona winked as she slid in next to Saul. "And a few of his elves."

"I can't pay for this."

"I know it's easier for you to give than receive." Leona removed the wrapper from a straw. "But you've given so much to this community. Surely you know how much giving blesses the giver. You wouldn't deny your friends that warm and fuzzy feeling so close to Christmas, would you?"

Before she could answer, Angus set a plate before her. Perfectly crisped fries and a burger topped with all of Ruthie's favorite condiments.

He gave his grandmother a smile and delivered her standard line, the one she always said to customers—back when she had customers. "Don't let those fries get cold." Proud of all he'd managed to pull off to surprise her, he spun on his heels and headed back to man the grill and fill a stack of orders.

Santa?

There had been more than a bit of paint and upholstering going on around here while she was gone. There had been an infusion of life.

Ruthie picked up a fry and pointed it at Leona. "Least I could do is bake this Santa and his elves a pie—"

The sound of a bell jangling turned Ruthie's attention to the door. A thin man in a red suit stepped in, his head lowered against the wind.

"Santa's here!" The boy who'd been sucking down Etta May's milkshake, snatched the pickled crab apple from the mound of whipped cream, jumped from his bar stool, and ran to the door.

"It's Santa." All the children shouted. They wiggled off their seats and out of their booths, then ran to greet the skinniest Santa she'd ever seen.

"Say it, Santa," a little girl squealed. "Say ho, ho, ho."

Santa set his pack by the door then he wiped his scuffed army boots on the mat. "Ho. Ho. Ho." He opened his arms and scooped in the swarm of children, laughing at their delight.

His beard was real.

His suit was real.

His ability to stop Ruthie's heart cold was real.

Ruthie dropped her crispy fry. "*Earl Dean* is Roxie's Santa?" Steam churned her words out so hot they burned her tongue. "Why don't you just give the jerk a pair of angel wings and stick him on top of the nativity float while you're at it?"

Chapter Thirteen

Leona

"But Roxie, I think your surgeon would agree with me that you should let Tom drive the combine," Leona pleaded over the phone. "At least, let me check with Maddie. See what she thinks about you driving heavy machinery." This last push to keep Roxie on the road to recovery was met with silence followed by a decisive click and dead air.

Leona slipped her phone into her robe pocket. She poured two cups of coffee and carried them to the couch where Saul sat watching the morning news.

Saul took the cup she offered. "Weather forecast looks good for parade day." His eyes narrowed when he saw her face. "But I see a storm brewing."

Not wanting to address her frustration over Roxie's reluctance to let her smother her with concern, she nodded toward the extended forecast scrolling on the flatscreen. "This is Texas. Weather can change on a dime."

"We can't control everything." He patted the seat beside him. "Roxie feeling better?"

"Who really knows?" Leona confessed. "According to her, she's more than capable of driving a combine in the parade."

"Is that why you didn't sleep again last night?"

"I paced in my socks."

"Might as well have been an elephant wearing tap shoes with all that guilt you're carrying."

"J.D. used to say that if it weren't for guilt trips, I'd never go anywhere."

Saul drew her close and planted a kiss on her temple. "What other horrible shortcomings are you guilty of now, my love?"

They'd always been free to talk about the pieces of their past lives, both the precious and the hard times they'd experienced, especially the dark days that followed the loss of their first spouses. Grief affected everyone differently. When J.D. died, she was terrified, afraid his absence would reveal every single one of her failings. When Saul lost his wife to cancer, he became sullen and withdrawn. Why hadn't she taken her newfound understanding of loss and applied its pain to Ruthie's reaction?

Maybe it was because Earl Dean hadn't died. He'd just abandoned his family. *Just abandoned his family.* What Ruthie's ex-husband had done was no small thing.

If J.D. had left her instead of dying, she would have had this secret hope in the back of her mind that one day he would come home, and they would find a way to reconcile. No matter how badly his actions may have hurt. But from watching Ruthie interact with Earl Dean, Leona could see how hoping could hurt worse than death. In Ruthie's mind, she'd declared Earl Dean dead years ago. It was the only way to let go of the pain of hope. It was asking a lot to expect Ruthie to wrap her head around the fact that her husband had been resurrected from the very grave where she'd buried her love for him. And with no warning!

Leona glanced at the paint cans, posters, and jars of pickles heaped high on her dining table. Saul had warned her about meddling in other's affairs. "This whole mess is my fault."

"Leona, the parade is a good idea." Saul knew the mess to which she was referring, but he was too much of a gentleman to say I told you so. "The excitement you've generated with you newspaper ads and digital articles has already increased local involvement and given the businesses along Main Street a boost, including yours."

Saul was right. An unexpected serendipity of the parade had been that the *Messenger* was on track to turn a profit this month, a fact that she hoped offered Ivan some relief from his worries of selling her a failing business.

"But if it hadn't been for the parade, I wouldn't have pushed Roxie to expedite her surgery or pushed Earl Dean on Ruthie."

"Maybe." One of Saul's eyebrows cocked in doubt. "At heart, you're an incurable romantic."

"Is it a crime to want my friends to be happy and healthy?"

Saul smiled, but he didn't remind her that she'd taken off again on her well-worn guilty path. "Nobody pushes Roxie or Ruthie around."

"True that." The only time Leona had been granted a peek beneath Ruthie's tough exterior was after Angus turned up. Ruthie took him in and made him family without batting an eye. Proof that Ruthie had a big heart under that apron of hers. Maybe, given the right circumstances, there was more love left in Ruthie than she believed. "But someone has to push Ruthie's wheelchair while I take Roxie for her radiation treatments."

Saul studied her with those legal-eagle eyes of his. "And you're thinking, why not Earl Dean?"

Leona shook her head. "You can't expect me to be in two places at once."

"Technically, Roxie has Tom and Ruthie has Angus."

"Tom has to step in and run the parts store, and Angus has more than he can do helping me with the paper and trying to run the diner at the same time. But both these fine men are going to drop if they continue to run businesses *and* care for their sick loved ones. The doctor said it would take at least a month for Ruthie to get back on her feet and gain enough strength to manage the diner on her own. And no one can predict exactly how Roxie will hold up to her treatments."

"I don't like the look in your eyes."

Leona waved off the implication she was overstepping. "Saul, the solution is simple. We simply must help Ruthie and Earl Dean patch things—"

"There's no *we* here." Saul set his cup on the coffee table and took her hands in his. "This old hurt is between Ruthie and Earl Dean."

"Maybe I could convince her to allow Earl Dean to cook on parade day, then—"

"Then you wouldn't have to feel guilty about talking Roxie into hiring Earl Dean to play Santa and giving the old man a reason to stick around." Saul stood and picked up his cup. "May I remind you that you launched into this whole parade business to help Roxie foot her medical bills?"

"And to keep the newspaper's doors open," she confessed.

"That's the trouble with good intentions. They often blur lines that shouldn't be crossed."

Maybe she was blurring the lines. True her concern for Roxie should have nothing to do with her desire to see Ruthie financially secure, but these two women had been instrumental in rallying the community to stand behind her in her hour of need. How could she desert them or the town of Mt. Hope now? In all good conscience, she could not stand by and do nothing.

"I feel like there's more to Ruthie and Earl Dean's story." Was she justifying her actions or yielding to the driving force building like a storm inside of her? Either way, she was in too deep to back out now. "Earl Dean seems like such a good man. He worked for hours painting and fixing up the diner . . . and did it without accepting a nickel in payment."

"Time mellows us all." Saul looked deep into her eyes then released her hands. "You don't know how he was before he left, or what drove him to make the choices he did."

"That's it. You're brilliant, Saul Levy." Leona kissed his cheek.

"Something tells me I just stepped into a trap."

She wrapped her arms around his neck and kissed him until she felt his resistance melt. "I agree that we should do a little background detective work."

He peeled free of her arms. "When you say *we,* I get the distinct impression you mean *me*?"

"I'll do everything I can, but I will need your help." Leona couldn't help but smile at the Lord's provision. Since their marriage, she'd seen God's wisdom in sending her this challenging man. What if the backbone she'd developed through her struggles had been the Lord's way of preparing her to accomplish his purpose? What if she, like Queen Esther, had been strategically maneuvered into this very position for such a time as this? How could she disappoint the Lord?

Every perfectionist tendency she thought she'd successfully buried suddenly rose from the dead. She pressed Saul further. "Surely you still have military contacts who owe you a favor."

"And what would I do with this favor?"

"Find out what happened to Earl Dean while he was serving."

"You want me to pull his service records?"

"It is our civic duty. He's working with children."

"He's working with children because you told Roxie he'd make the perfect Santa," Saul pointed out, annoyance creeping into his voice. "According to all accounts of the whole the Prodigal-is-back incident, the man just stepped into the Koffee Kup for coffee. You have no proof that *said* man came home to make amends."

"If we're talking legalese"—Leona gathered their mugs and marched to the sink— "*Said* man could have acquired free coffee hanging around outside the Quick Mart. However, *said* man came to the diner for a reason."

Saul raised an eyebrow, obviously impressed at her rebuttal. "Have you or have you not expressed concern that *said* man might be ill."

She poured cold coffee down the drain. "Earl Dean is a little shaky on his feet, but who isn't at his age? I don't think he came back in hopes Ruthie would take care of him. I think Earl Dean Crouch wants to make amends for the hurt he's caused, especially to Ruthie."

Saul came up behind her. He slid his arms around her waist and leaned in close enough for his mustache to nuzzle her neck, a non-courtroom tactic he'd used to calm her whenever they danced on the dock. "Leona, trying to fix the years of struggle and pain Earl Dean's abandonment inflicted on Ruthie is well above my pay grade and yours."

She wheeled. "Did you see the way he looks at Ruthie?"

Saul sighed, "Same way I look at you." He took a step back and pulled out his phone.

"What are you doing?"

"Finding out if Earl Dean Crouch has an honorable discharge from the U.S. military." Saul scrolled through his contact list. "If so, he's entitled to a wide variety of veteran benefits." Saul peered over his glasses. "I'll help you get the man back on his feet, but I draw the line at helping you get his feet back under Ruthie's table."

Leona smiled. "Deal." She threw her arms around her husband's neck again. "You're a keeper, Saul Levy." But even as she held him tight, she knew Ruthie held her grudges tighter. She and the Lord had their work cut out for them.

Chapter Fourteen

Ruthie

"You're supposed to be resting, MeMaw." Angus pushed Ruthie's wheelchair away from the cash register and parked her at a table facing the street. "I can do the chores while the bacon is frying."

"I'm not dead." She reached into a basket of forks still hot from the dishwasher. "I can still roll silverware and marry ketchup bottles." She stacked a knife, fork, and spoon in the middle of a big paper napkin. "Besides, you need to stay close to the grill. Pork will turn to charcoal if you don't stay on it." A couple of quick turns and a tuck of the napkin, and the silverware bundle was complete. "Good bacon ain't cheap."

"I've watched you fry bacon for years." Angus took her neatly rolled bundle and laid it in the basket he insisted they store inside the ridiculously large welcome podium. "It's not that hard once you get a rhythm going."

She pointed a fork at him. "You're a stubborn one, Angus Freestone."

Quick as a wink, he relieved her of the fork, added a knife and spoon, then spun his own neat silverware bundle. "Wonder who I get that from?"

Before she could comment on the value of inheriting her ability to stick to her guns, a flash of red drew Angus's gaze to the window and the activity going on in front of Brewer's Auto & Tractor Parts.

"Looks like Roxie's feeling better and back in the store."

Ruthie shifted her gaze toward the parts store. "Whatcha mean, looks like Roxie's feeling better?"

"She was out for a few days while you were in rehab. Left Tom to run everything. Which seems odd that she'd take time off right when business started to pick up over at the parts store." Angus finished the bundle in his hand, then followed her intent focus. "She and Ed are starting early."

It was strange seeing Tom trail after Roxie like a worried mother hen, which would have been a warning flag had she not had her focused shifted to what Angus had just called his grandfather. "Ed?"

"Short for Earl Dean."

"What happened to calling him PePaw?"

"No point getting attached if he's not staying around." Angus had tried to disguise the longing in his voice, but Ruthie's perceptivity hadn't been damaged in the fall.

She knew she had a part in this new hole life had punched in his hope of having a real family. Across the street, a thin man with tattered backpack strapped over a red velvet suit helped the paler-than-usual owner of Brewer Auto & Tractor Parts scoot a wooden rocking chair along the sidewalk. If protecting Angus from a bigger hurt meant letting him experience a little hurt now, then that's what she'd have to do.

"What does he keep in that backpack?" Ruthie squeezed the fork in her fist. "He could be an ax murderer for all we know."

"MeMaw, you don't really think Ed is an ax murderer."

"I think he's a low-down, lying skunk, but no, the Earl Dean I knew wouldn't hurt a fly. That's why fighting in the war was so hard on him."

"I'd like to ask him about his time in the military."

"He's Santa," she snorted. "You can ask him for anything, right?"

"I guess."

"Then while you're asking for the impossible, which telling you the truth about his service would be, why don't you ask him to make our lease payment?" She clapped her hand to her mouth, but it was too late. She hadn't meant to let that slip. "I mean . . ."

"You don't have to hide the state of our finances, MeMaw. It's not rocket science. No customers. No money in our pockets."

"Well, then you know we can't afford to burn the bacon." She nodded toward the sizzle coming from behind the counter. "Best get back to cookin'."

"It's going to be okay, MeMaw. God's got us."

She patted his hand. "'Course he does."

After Angus returned to the grill, Ruthie tried to act like she believed God would provide. She busied herself rolling silverware like a woman who did not hang her future on the Santa setting up shop in front of the parts store across the street. But try as she might, she couldn't keep her eyes on her own business.

The Story sisters trailed behind Earl Dean and Roxie. Nola Gay had twisted her snowy hair into a bun at the nape of her neck. She wore a white apron over a long red dress and carried a basket of pickle jars like she was Mrs. Claus preparing to feed hungry elves. Etta May was decked out in a pointy elf's hat, a checkered top that came to the knees of her bright green tights. The sweet old lady had her own basket of pickles slung over her arm.

The wind snatched Etta May's hat. As she turned to catch it, a canning jar jostled from the basket and crashed on the sidewalk. For a second, Etta May's face puckered. Nola Gay set her basket among the pieces of broken glass and scurried after her sister's hat.

Earl Dean hadn't taken the time to stuff his suit with pillows. Red velvet hung from his thin frame. He saw what happened, then sprinted after the two sisters who chased after the hat. His backpack bounced on his back like an unhinged camel's hump. Just as the hat somersaulted toward the wet gutter, Earl Dean pulled ahead of the old women and snatched it up. Etta May and Nola Gay laughed and patted his shoulder like they were so proud of their old friend. Which, technically they were. Old friends. The twins had been first in line for breakfast the day she and Earl Dean officially opened the diner.

Ancient longings clawed at Ruthie's heart. Useless longings. She couldn't imagine living as carefree as those three old birds. She had long since lost the ability to believe life could be fun. She would never have the luxury of playing Mrs. Claus.

She hadn't noticed Angus had rejoined her at the table until she heard him drop the last rolled silverware set into the basket. "Guess the break in the weather has Roxie hoping to take advantage of offering visits with Santa."

Ruthie unscrewed the lid from a ketchup bottle. "Good for her." She flipped the half-empty bottle over and set it atop another equally empty ketchup bottle.

When she looked up, a stranger dressed in a dirty army jacket was drifting toward the jolly group across the street. "Doubt that one will buy much," Ruthie muttered.

Roxie turned and greeted the stranger like he was her best customer. Then she turned and leaned in close to Earl Dean's ear. Whatever that parts woman had whispered, she had Earl Dean rubbing his hands together and scurrying over to the Santa chair.

The Story sisters took their place on either side of Santa, their baskets draped over their arms and Etta May holding on to her hat. Earl Dean noticed the drifter hanging back and motioned him forward.

The man removed his worn military cap. Earl Dean offered the man a hearty handshake then started chatting with the fellow like they were long-lost friends. Ruthie squinted, trying to read Earl Dean's lips but couldn't make out what tall tale Earl Dean was spewing. The man nodded as if he agreed with every word coming out of Earl Dean's mouth. Then Earl Dean looked down at the man's worn-out boots. The man shook his head. Earl Dean didn't hesitate. He plopped into the Santa rocker and quickly removed the new boots the pastor had dug out of the church's benevolence closet.

Ruthie and Angus both leaned forward. Earl Dean wiggled the toes poking through his socks and pointed at the other man's boots. The man shook his head, but Earl Dean thrust his new boots toward the man.

Angus pushed his face up against the window glass. "Ed's going to give that man his new boots." The admiration lacing his declaration grated on Ruthie like nails on a chalkboard.

"You don't know that," she snapped.

"Look." Angus pointed, wonder sparkling in eyes blind to truth. "Ed's putting on the man's old boots."

"It's easy to be benevolent when it doesn't cost you anything," Ruthie growled. "He'd have given away the roof I'd slaved to keep over our heads."

Angus pulled out his phone. "I need to get a picture of this for Ivan. It would make a great human-interest story for the paper." He clicked off a few shots. As he scrolled back through them, astounded disbelief lit his face. "When I was living on the road, I never met anyone who would have done that for me."

Jealousy stabbed her heart. "You've got a roof over your head now because I have always sacrificed for my family."

"I know, MeMaw." Angus tapped around on his phone without looking at her. "And I'm grateful."

Grateful, just not impressed enough to look her in the eye and express his gratitude like her sacrifice had meant something to him.

It irked her that Earl Dean had so easily left everything of importance behind . . . everything but that easy-going charm of his. It irked her that his charisma was a magic potion people seemed eager to swallow. One sip of his good nature and they were all too willing to forgive him any wrongs. Then, to add insult to injury, it really irked her that people seemed to bend over backward to help him keep living his footloose and fancy-free life. She, on the other hand, had stayed chained to her responsibilities. Worked hard. Done all of it without accepting a single offer of help from anyone. And somewhere along the line, she'd exchanged her pleasant personality for a barn sour one.

"Barn sour?" Angus asked, his head cocked in her direction.

Ruthie blinked, "What?"

"You just blurted out barn sour."

She hadn't meant to speak her self-condemnation out loud, but apparently the truth of how she felt about herself refused to be penned in any longer. "My daddy used to say that when animals are kept shut up too long, they become listless and fail to thrive . . . he called them barn sour."

"I don't understand."

She loved this grandson of hers. Thought he was smarter than she'd ever be. But for all his learning, he sure could be thick headed.

She knew people called her Ruthie *Grouch* behind her back. Didn't Angus weary of her grumpy ways? She sure did. Maybe Angus really did appreciate all she'd done for him and was choosing to give her the benefit of the doubt. Either way, she was grateful life hadn't soured him. And she was going to do everything in her power to see that it never did. Even if it meant keeping him away from the influences of his grandfather.

She unscrewed the cap on another ketchup bottle. "That man playing like he's Santa Claus, he's just a—"

"Oh no." Angus thrust his phone at her. "Call Charlie." He burst out the diner's front door and shot across the street.

Ruthie strained her eyes to locate the emergency that had prompted Angus to order an ambulance as he left her. Across the street, she noticed Nola Gay, Etta May, and Roxie swarming a crumpled heap of red velvet on the sidewalk. A man in a Santa suit lay face down, his pack protruding from his back like a lone mountain peak.

"Earl Dean!" she shouted as if he could have heard her through the thick plate glass.

Earl Dean didn't move.

Hands shaking, Ruthie dialed the ambulance.

A few minutes later, Main Street was all sirens and flashing lights. Charlie parked his vehicle so that it completely obscured Ruthie's view of Earl Dean. Charlie jumped out, grabbed his medical bag, then ran.

What if Earl Dean died?

For years, she'd been telling herself that he *was* dead. It made all those long and lonely nights easier to think he wanted to come back to her but couldn't cross the chasm between life and death.

Now, knowing that he really might die, she couldn't breathe.

Ruthie tried to push back from the table. But her one good hand didn't have enough strength to move her wheelchair. She couldn't let Angus go through this alone. Let him watch one more person disappear from his life. He'd never forgive her for not forgiving Earl Dean on his deathbed.

Ruthie scrolled through Angus's contacts until she found Leona's number. "This is Ruthie. You at the newspaper office?"

"Not yet," Leona said. "Why are you calling me on Angus's phone?"

"There's been an accident."

"Are you two, okay?"

"I am," Ruthie said. "But I'm worried about Angus."

Ruthie proceeded to tell Leona what she thought had happened across the street. She had to admit that she'd been so busy hating Earl Dean that she hadn't actually seen him go down. "Can David come? Get my Angus out of there?"

"I'll call him," Leona said. "Sit tight, Ruthie."

Chapter Fifteen

Ruthie

The moment Ruthie clicked off the call with Leona, the sharp tang of burning meat hit her nostrils. "The bacon!"

She yelled for Angus, but he'd inserted himself too deep into the action happening in front of Brewer's. He'd never hear her over the noise of the ambulance siren and the curious crowd pressing in around the down-and-out Santa.

Ruthie picked up the cell phone to call Angus, then realized he'd left his phone with her.

If she wanted the bacon saved, she'd have to figure out how to do it herself. She unlocked the brake of her wheelchair, placed her good palm against the table, and gave herself the hardest backward shove she could muster. Her wheelchair crashed into a dining chair behind her and sent it toppling. There was no time to tidy up *and* save her bacon.

Cranking one wheel of her chair with her good hand, Ruthie huffed her way across the dining room. Bacon popped and hissed on the grill. She had only seconds before several pounds of prime pork went up in smoke. As she worked her way around the counter, the meat in the center of the grill was already beginning to blacken. Any minute, she could have another fire. If she had to call the volunteer fire department, Ivan would have no choice but to add her incident to Earl Dean's. The only thing worse than being on the front page of the *Messenger* would be to have her photo side by side with the charming new Santa in town.

Ruthie fumbled with the grill's knobs, but the cast on her wrist made it difficult to know if she'd managed to turn them completely off. Even if she had, the grill was so hot it would be at least five minutes before it cooled enough to stop cooking. She still needed to remove the bacon.

Unfortunately, Angus had returned her long spatula to the hook that hung over the grill.

Ruthie strained.

Too high.

The long wooden spoon she used to scrape every drop of gravy from the cans protruded from the sink. She grabbed the spoon and used it like a bat to knock the spatula free. The metal utensil flew off the hook and clattered to the floor.

Now what?

She leaned forward in her chair, stretching her unbroken arm as far as possible. The spatula remained out of reach.

Bacon sizzled at her eye level.

She scooted to the edge of her seat and used the lip of the cast on her foot to hook the spatula and send it flying. The spatula handle caught on the wheel of her chair. She was able to reach and pry it free. Without taking time to clean it off, she slid the spatula's flat end under the bacon strips nearest the front edge of the grill.

Now that she had a load of charred bacon balanced on the tip of her utensil, what was she going to do with it? Normally, she would grab a plate from the rack and flip the load without losing a strip. But the plates were stored above the grill.

The bacon toward the back of the grill was beginning to smoke.

She had to make a choice. Sacrifice the bacon or her diner.

With a flick of her good wrist, Ruthie flipped hot bacon onto the Formica countertop. She'd help Angus clean up the mess later.

Now to remove the rest of the bacon.

Heat seared the tender inside flesh of Ruthie's good arm as she stretched as far as she could.

Almost there. Just. A. Little. Further.

No matter how hard she tried, she couldn't reach the bacon toward the back of the grill. If she could raise up on her good leg, just long enough to get the flat end of the spatula behind the meat and push it forward, she might ...

She pushed up. But the strength in her good arm wasn't enough to balance the weight of two heavy casts. The wheelchair tipped, and before she could stop herself from falling, Ruthie landed on her back with a bone-jarring thud, immediately followed by the crushing weight of the wheelchair. The chair's handles pinned her head to the cold black and white tiles. Wheels spun above her like planets rotating among the stars in her eyes. When she tried to move, pain shot through her entire body.

The bell above the door sounded in her head.

"MeMaw!" Angus flew around the counter. He lifted the chair off her chest. "Are you alright?"

"Get the bacon!" She tugged at the hem of her dress that was up around her neck. "Then get me upright, Angus, before anyone sees me flailing like a turtle on its back."

"Too late." Earl Dean's gravelly voice sent shards of anger peppered with relief coursing through Ruthie's veins.

Ruthie squirmed until her eyes laid a bead on the man peering over the counter. "Thought you were busy dying on the sidewalk, old man."

"Me too," Earl Dean admitted in a low weary voice.

"His sugar dropped." Angus eased his arm under her and gently lifted her to a sitting position. "You okay."

"Yes." Ruthie took a deep breath. When her equilibrium shifted back into place, she nodded toward Earl Dean. "How did he get back on his feet so fast?"

"Charlie gave him orange juice, but says he needs a good meal."

"You mean *free* meal," Ruthie snapped, rubbing the back of her head.

"I can pay." Earl Dean pulled a ten-dollar bill from the pocket of his red suit. "Mrs. Brewer gave me an advance." He slapped it on the counter. "I remember that you make a mighty mean biscuit."

How dare he remember anything about her. "Then you should also remember all the work that goes into making them biscuits."

Angus tugged her arms. "I'm going to need help to get you up."

"Here." Earl Dean eased himself around the counter. "Allow me."

Ruthie batted at him with the cast on her arm. "Don't you touch me, Earl Dean Crouch."

"MeMaw," Angus said. "Either you let Ed help us out, or I'm going to have to call Charlie." He nodded toward the window. "You've never kept a crowd waiting on breakfast."

Angus was right. In all her years of running this business, she'd not missed a day that she was not open and ready to go before the first hungry mouth arrived.

"Crowd?" She hadn't had a crowd at breakfast since the council met at her diner. She glanced over her shoulder and saw people lined up outside her diner window. Paying customers were gifts she had no choice but to accept. "Oh, all right," she huffed. "But you mind where you put your hands, Earl Dean."

"You know I will." Earl Dean slid his arms under hers. His soft beard tickled her neck and his warm breath sent tingles racing through Ruthie's limp limbs. Before she could tell Angus to tell Earl Dean to back away and leave her be, Earl Dean told Angus, "You grab her hands, son. Lift on three."

The first time she and Earl Dean ever touched was the first time she'd felt these very same tingles. It had been years since she'd let herself remember that magical moment Earl Dean proposed beside the lake.

Not once while she was going on about her dreams of one day owning this diner while they sucked down root beer floats in the back booth had Earl Dean even tried to hold her hand, let alone kiss her. She worried he found her plain and boring. So, that day he took her fishing at the lake, she asked him straight out why he stuck around.

He said he'd never had a reason to stay in one place . . . not until now. Then he leaned his fishing pole against the tree and dropped to one knee. Only when she said yes, did he take her in his arms and kiss her . . . a kiss she'd never forget.

Where had that Earl Dean gone?

Ruthie sank into her chair, tingles still tangled in her memories. "Get the door unlocked, Angus. I'll start cleaning up this bacon mess."

"You'll do no such thing." Earl Dean took hold of the handles of her wheelchair. "If I hadn't caused such a ruckus, Angus would have been tending the grill." He pushed Ruthie's wheelchair out from behind the counter. "This mess is mine to clean up."

"You're not touching another thing in *my* diner."

"Look at that crowd." Earl Dean nodded toward the window. "Angus can't handle that kind of backup on his own. Let me help him."

Several faces peered through the new glass. Children shouted, "There's Santa."

Much as she hated to admit anything good could possibly come for Earl Dean suddenly turning up, it had been a long time since she'd seen this many people lined up to get in her diner. "I can work the door."

"That fall shook you pretty good," Earl Dean said. "The more you rest, the sooner you'll be back on your feet."

"The door," she insisted.

"Still as stubborn as ever I see." He pushed her to the welcome podium, then came around and stood in front of her. "Can you still smile?" Who did he think he was telling her what she needed to do when he needed to apologize for hurting her like he did and add thirty pounds if he was going to fill out that Santa suit? The tremor in his hands reminded her that Charlie had said he should eat something.

If Earl Dean thought slinging a little hash instead of taking care of his health would make up for the years she'd had to manage everything all by herself, he must have hit his head during his fall. Seeing Earl Dean slaving over a hot grill would be sweet revenge. But seeing him so thin and worn left her little appetite for dishing out the spite he deserved.

"I'll smile after you eat something, old man."

A pleased grin tugged the corner of his mouth. "You really do care, don't you, Ruthie."

Ruthie pulled a stack of menus from the shelf behind the podium. "Just because I don't want you falling on my grill and causing another scene doesn't mean I give a hoot or a holler what happens to you, Earl Dean." She tapped the menus on the podium to even them out. "Get some food in that belly of yours before you touch my grill."

He gave her a full-on toothy grin . . . well, what was left of his teeth, and a little mock salute. "Will do."

She couldn't help but wonder about the demons he'd wrestled and how he'd managed to keep himself alive living on the road. But since he'd chosen not to make his problems her problems, she'd make sure he did not become her problem.

"Once this breakfast rush is over," she said steering her unexpected sense of concern back into the shed of her heart." "You're taking that ratty bag of yours and hitting the road. Understand, Earl Dean?"

"Santa never stays any one place too long." He swallowed hard and cast a sideways glance at Angus. "Every kid knows that."

"Why did you come back, Earl Dean?" The fall must have jarred loosed the question she'd pondered since his return because it blurted out before she could stop it. "Why now?"

Before he could answer, Angus unlocked the front door and people streamed inside. What did his answer matter anyway? Earl Dean had been a wanderer when she met him. She'd been wrong to think she could change him then, and she was way too old and way too tired to try and change him now.

"The sooner you go, the better it will be for . . ." she gulped.

"Angus." Earl Dean finished her sentence, saving her the pain of having to admit that it would be better for her as well.

"Right." Ruthie let her gaze drift to the young man whistling at the grill. Deny it all she wanted, but that boy was as much a part of Earl Dean as he was a part of her. "For Angus."

She could ride her high horse into the sunset, but she could never look at Angus again and say that nothing good had come from her loving this man posing as Santa.

CHAPTER SIXTEEN

Ruthie

Earl Dean tapped the bell above the grill, "Order up." His Santa cap rode low over his eyes and his red sleeves were rolled to his bony elbows. "Angus, I think we may need to start another pot of coffee."

Angus slid three plates filled with grits, bacon, biscuits, and gravy onto one arm. "On it, Ed."

A few minutes later, Angus brought Ruthie a bowl of biscuits and gravy. She took a bite. The delicious taste that hit her tongue was a mixture of familiar and heavenly.

She looked up at Angus's anxious face. "What's this?"

"*Homemade* gravy," he beamed.

"What's wrong with the canned gravy?"

"Ran out an hour ago."

"Nobody told me."

"You've been busy manning the door." Angus waited, staring at her with his eyes all expectant. "Well . . ."

"Well, what?"

"Gravy's good, isn't it?"

She tasted another spoonful of the creamy sauce. Chunks of crispy sausage complimented the splash of bacon grease and the perfect dash of black pepper. She nodded toward the skinny Santa whizzing around behind the counter. "I never said Earl Dean couldn't cook."

Angus leaned in close. "Let's ask him to stay." The idea of finally having a family was a chain pulling Angus farther and farther from his dreams.

She could not let that happen. "Angus—"

"Ed said he'd sure like to teach me how to fish."

"Until you learn how to swim, I don't want you anywhere near the water."

"Well, Ed can probably teach me that too?"

It would be easier to try to nail down the wind than to keep Earl Dean in one place long enough to teach anyone anything. "Earl Dean says he'll do lots of things." Ruthie passed her bowl back to Angus. "Believe him, and you'll get your heart broken."

The breakfast rush continued much longer than expected. Word that Santa was cooking at the Koffee Kup shifted the crowd from Roxie's to the diner. Ruthie felt a pang of guilt. Roxie looked pale. Probably worried sick about medical bills piling up. Roxie needed the business as much as she did. Maybe she could spell Earl Dean and send him back to Roxie's. Having Santa across the street might push folks Roxie's way after they had their bellies filled.

She seated a family of four at the next empty table, but as she started for the grill, she couldn't help but notice how well Angus and Earl Dean worked together. Like they'd been cut from the same bolt of cloth.

Earl Dean still knew his way around her kitchen. But Ruthie had only herself to blame for his comfort. In the years Earl Dean had been gone, she'd not rearranged a single utensil. He could easily set stuff to frying, boiling, mixing, and baking. He was comfortable as a man who'd simply stepped out for a quick smoke, stepped back in, and took up right where he'd left off.

Only he hadn't. He'd been gone forty years, she reminded herself. Forty long, lonely years.

Ruthie wheeled herself back to her welcome station. She'd send Earl Dean back to Roxie's once things slowed down a bit.

As the clock ticked toward noon, Ruthie realized that not a single order had been sent back to the grill. Customers she'd never seen before rubbed their bellies and added twenty-percent tips to their tabs. On their way out, they told Ruthie they'd be back. Food this good was worth the drive.

"Food this good," Ruthie muttered as she pushed in the heavy cash drawer. "Be sure and stop by Brewer's before you leave town. They've got several sales going on."

"We'll wait for Santa," they'd all said.

"The lunch regulars are fixin' to hit the door," she shouted toward the grill. "Earl Dean, I'll fry the chicken livers and burgers."

But he'd refused, saying it would be a shame to break the rhythm he and Angus had going. Unwilling to admit Earl Dean was as good at cooking as he was at playing Santa, Ruthie snatched up some clean rags and a spray bottle of disinfectant.

She'd barely gotten the pancake syrup wiped off the table at Leona and Saul's booth when the happy couple showed up for their regular lunch burgers.

"We'll have our usual," Leona told Ruthie as she slid into a recovered bench seat.

"After you put our order in, we'd like to talk to you," Saul added as he tucked into his side of the booth.

"About what?"

"It can wait until you have a minute to give this your full attention," Leona said.

"You're scaring me, but okay." Ruthie wheeled to the counter. "Booth four will have two burgers, well done. Lettuce and tomato on one. Cheese only on the other. Hold the fries. Two sweet teas." Earl Dean lifted his spatula in acknowledgement but didn't stop to write it down. "You got that, Earl Dean?"

He tossed two frozen patties on the grill and hit them with a generous dash of salt and pepper. "Got it."

"I'd feel better if you wrote down every order."

He turned his head. "Never wrote down an order in my life."

There were many things he'd never done. Stick around being one of them.

But Ruthie pushed back from the counter without reiterating that point. Steam building inside her, she rolled her chair to Leona and Saul's booth.

"If you want to talk about how I should take that man back, then you're wasting your breath."

"Ruthie," Leona said, her voice low. "I was wrong to push him on you."

"Never a truer word spoken."

"Ruthie," Leona glanced toward the grill then leaned toward the wheelchair. "I had Saul do a little digging into Earl Dean's military record."

All sorts of things spun in Ruthie's mind. The time had long passed for her interest in Earl Dean's military record. He'd not said two words about his time in Vietnam and that could only mean one thing: it wasn't good. And if that was the case, whatever he'd done seemed like his story to tell.

She shook her head. "I don't—"

Leona held up her palm. "Private Earl Dean Crouch was—"

Howard Davis huffed up to the table. "Leona, we need to talk."

"Can it wait, Howard?" Leona asked. "We're kind of busy here."

"If you want your floats pulled by shiny pickups, then I need to know how many I need to have detailed." The used car salesman ignored Leona and rambled on about pickup trucks and float weight approximations.

Ruthie used the interruption as an opportunity to retreat to the welcome station. Did she really want to know about what horrible things Private Earl Dean Crouch might have done in the jungle...how he'd lived with the guilt? All she really wanted to know was what he'd done with his life since. And she was the one who'd have to kick that hornet's nest.

Try as she might, she could not keep her gaze from wandering over to the grill.

The white ball on the tip of Earl Dean's red Santa hat bobbed as he waltzed from one end of the grill to the other, whistling Christmas tunes through his scattered teeth. Angus delivered onion rings and burgers to the tables in record time. The two men were an instant and efficient team.

"Earl Dean's doing a fantastic job, Ruthie." Leona slid a twenty into Ruthie's outstretched palm on her way out the door. "Sorry we didn't get to finish our conversation. I can come back on my break."

Ruthie waved off her offer, pretty sure she didn't really want answers after all. "Earl Dean is a snowflake, Leona." She slipped the big bill under the divider in the drawer. "Squeeze him too tight and he'll melt away."

CHAPTER SEVENTEEN

Ruthie

Once the lunch crowd had cleared, Angus and Earl Dean got to work setting up the diner for tomorrow's big Christmas parade crowd. While Earl Dean emptied the dishwasher and stacked all the clean plates in the rack above the grill, she and Angus took the supply list Earl Dean had scribbled on a napkin and checked the pantry.

Empty.

Ruthie returned to the cash drawer and counted out the day's take. If Angus did some bargain hunting, they might manage to feed a hundred folks.

Angus slipped into his jacket. "I'm going to run to the grocery store before Ed and I go fishing." He kissed Ruthie on the cheek.

"Fishing?" Ruthie shot Earl Dean a glare. "Has *my* boy told you he can't swim?"

Earl Dean flinched at her emphasis on *my* boy but a couple of days frying burgers with Angus did not make him a grandfather deserving of the hope she saw on her grandson's face.

"It's too cold for swimming." Earl Dean screwed the cap on a full pepper shaker. "We're just going to stand on the bank, cast a couple of lines, and catch a little fresh air, Ruthie." He set the pepper shaker near the shiny-clean grill. "Won't be gone long."

"That's what you said the last time you took out."

"MeMaw—"

Earl Dean held up a palm to silence Angus. "I deserved that, boy." Earl Dean stood before her, shaky hand raised like a defendant swearing to tell the truth, the whole truth, and nothing but the truth. "Your MeMaw is right. I did a real bad thing walking out on her like I did."

"But you're sorry, right, Ed?" Angus said.

Earl Dean's sad gaze sank a hook straight into Ruthie's heart. "More than you'll ever know."

"See, MeMaw?" Angus straightened his coat. "He's sorry."

She felt herself being reeled toward the truth of Earl Dean's statement. But it would take more than this half-felt apology to fix everything this man had broken. Promises. Trust. Her heart. Just to name a few.

Ruthie shoved the grocery list and crumpled dollar bills at Angus. "Better get yourself on to the store if you're going to get much fishing in before dark."

Being caught in the middle of this war flickered across Angus's face. He looked from Earl Dean to her, then acquiesced with a silent nod. "Mind if I take the truck?"

She slammed the cash drawer shut. "You know where I keep the keys."

Ruthie waited until she saw Angus drive her old F150 past the diner windows before she turned on Earl Dean. Part of her wanted to remind him that it was only by her good graces he wasn't sleeping under some overpass. Part of her wanted to ream him out. Tell him she didn't appreciate the pain he had brought to Angus. Part of her wanted to ... she wasn't sure what the broken part of her wanted.

Instead, she wheeled toward the counter and said, "You take time to eat anything?"

He shook his head. "That lunch crowd was something. They had me hopping."

She should give him a bit of credit. Things had always been better when he was around, but she didn't dare let herself get used to his help. He'd be gone again soon. The Christmas traffic would dry up, and then things would seem even bleaker than they had a few days ago.

"I've handled worse," she said.

Earl Dean peered at the nearly empty shelves in the pie display case. "Mind if I help myself to a spoonful of that apple pie?"

"No such thing as a spoonful of pie in *my* diner," Ruthie said. "Besides, I think pie is the last thing a diabetic like you needs."

Earl Dean lifted the apron over his head and hung it on the hook. "Life's too short to pass up a good piece of pie." He slid open the glass case and pulled out the pie tin. "This is the last of the apple."

"Folks will have to learn to eat cake." Ruthie held up her casted arm. "Gonna be a few weeks before I can roll crust."

"I'm happy to bake a few pies, if that will—"

"Make up for leaving me and Ruby?"

"Ruby." He whispered their daughter's name. "Wish I'd known her."

"Wishin' don't make it so."

His face crumpled like her words had slapped him. He turned and silently made his way to the Bunn. Took down two mugs and filled them with coffee. He shuffled to the table where she sat, proud and stiff and guilty.

"I am sorry, Ruthie." Steam rose from the cup he shakily set before her. "Truly, I am." He sank into the chair on the opposite side of the table. "I'm not trying to take Angus from you."

Instead of asking him to explain his motives or his shaky hands, she let her mind wander back to before the war. To before the time when things changed between them. Back to the time when they'd shared everything about running this diner. In those days, she'd loved the lull after the lunch crowd cleared out. They'd close the diner and take themselves a little break. She'd cut two huge pieces of pie while Earl Dean filled two cups with the last of the coffee. Earl Dean would talk of joining the military so he could see the world. She'd cut lard into flour. She'd been so busy perfecting her pie crusts that she'd failed to see they were two different people. Always would be.

The sound of Earl Dean's fork scraping for the last crumbs of pie crust brought Ruthie back to the present. She cupped the mug and pondered the strength of her courage as she watched him fork sugary bites to the mouth she used to kiss. If she asked the question that had burned a hole in her innards for years, she might not like the answer. It'd been easier to push the question aside when Earl Dean wasn't around to ask.

But here he was.

Sitting right in front of her.

If she didn't ask it now, it would be her own fault if she combusted from the inside out.

If she'd learned anything about herself these last forty years, she'd learned she was not a coward.

Ruthie steadied her grip on the coffee mug. "What happened overseas, Earl Dean?"

He took a swig of his coffee, swallowed hard, then raised his eyes to meet hers. If he was surprised by the question, his face didn't show it. "I done some things I wasn't proud of."

"It was war."

"But that don't make it any easier to sleep."

"I wish you would have talked to me about it." Ruthie ran her finger around the rim of her coffee mug. "Let me help you."

His pleading gazed fixed on her. "I'd always intended to come back to you and our baby." Something akin to the trust they used to share passed between their locked gazes. "When I was once again the man you deserved."

"What kind of man did you think I deserved?"

He stroked his beard. "One better than me."

"Are you that kind of man now?"

"I'm good as I'm gonna get, Ruthie." He lowered his head and used the flat of his fork to collect the last flakes of crust. "According to the docs at the VA hospital, the diabetes and smoking has taken a toll on my lungs."

This news did not anger her in the same way suspicion had when he first stepped through her door. Instead, a rare bolt of compassion shot straight through her heart. Anyone could see from his spindly arms and legs that this man was not the solid specimen of good health he'd been when he helped her drag in the diner's big grill years ago.

"This place is still half yours," she said, surprised voicing this admission hadn't killed her on the spot.

Earl Dean raised his head and studied her for a moment, his gaze neither surprised nor hopeful. "Owning a diner was always your dream, Ruthie. Not mine."

Although his tone was more regretful than combative, she bristled, ready to argue. To point out he was the one who wrote recipes and menu ideas on napkins. Then she remembered he was right.

She was the one who dragged him to the diner after the movie shows. She was the one who wanted to sit in the back booth and drink root beer floats. She was the one who'd said they should skip their honeymoon and hurry back and lease this place.

He'd wanted to spend their first year together restaurant hopping by day and walking along beautiful lakes to watch the moonlight dance on the water by night.

The forgotten truth of who they really were began to loosen its knot. Something cold and hard inside her began to thaw.

She reached for his hand. "You aren't the only one who's made mistakes, Earl Dean."

A tired grin cut a jagged swath in his beard. "Thank you, Ruthie. That's a kindness I don't deserve." He gave her hand a grateful squeeze, then pushed back from the table. "Think I'll clean the grease trap." He picked up his empty plate. "Don't want a grill fire on parade day."

Chaining Earl Dean Crouch to a six-days-a-week job would be like putting a firefly in a jar and expecting it to shine forever. They'd always been as different as black-eyed peas and navy beans. But, for the first time since Earl Dean left, Ruthie could see that their differences didn't mean they couldn't find a way back to their friendship.

Seeing the man she'd hated for so long for who he really was, she whispered, "Earl Dean."

He cocked his head. "Yes?"

"Angus needs a man to teach him how to fish." She offered a small smile. "I believe you're that man."

Chapter Eighteen

Ruthie

As the streetlights flickered on, Ruthie rolled her wheelchair to the diner window. She'd allowed Angus to close the diner after the lunch rush to give him and Earl plenty of daylight hours to fish. They'd asked her to come along, but she could tell they were both excited to have some private bonding time. So, she'd shelved the last of her reservations and said she'd finish wiping down the menus and filling bud vases with the red carnations Angus had splurged on at the grocery store. She and Earl agreed that Angus had made a wise purchase. The dining room, with its fresh coat of yellow paint and red upholstered booths, did feel more festive than it had in years.

Or maybe it was she who was feeling festive.

Agreement with Earl Dean felt far better than hate.

Her stomach rumbled. She checked the window and then the clock on the opposite wall. It'd been dark for over an hour. The wind had picked up and the temperature had dropped. Rain had turned to sleet. Angus and Earl Dean should have returned from their little fishing trip by now. She tried to phone Angus, but her call went immediately to voicemail. Angus had always answered her, even when he was in class.

She tried again. And again. And again.

Something was wrong.

She knew it in her bones.

Fingers shaking, she dialed the first name that came to mind. "Leona," she blurted before the woman even had a chance to say hello. "Help." She went on to rattle off that Earl Dean had taken Angus fishing at the lake. "Saul have lights on his boat?"

"He does."

"I hate to ask, but do you think Saul would take his boat out and see what's keeping them?"

"Do you know where on the lake they might be?"

Earl Dean hadn't said, but she knew exactly where he'd taken his grandson. "The western shore. There's a single tree that sits on a small rock ledge."

Leona repeated the description to her husband then came back on the line. "Saul knows the spot, Ruthie. It's across the lake from us. But I'm afraid, the wind has made the water too rough for Saul to take his boat out."

"Can he drive the lake road?"

"He's bundling himself up as we speak. I'll throw some blankets in his car." Leona's take-charge voice was a blanket of comfort. "I'll call David and ask him to meet the sheriff and launch a shoreline search party."

"Have David come get me."

"I think you need to stay put, Ruthie. Someone needs to be at the diner if ... I mean *when* they come home," Leona said. "I'm coming to sit with you until we have your fellows safely seated around your table."

Ruthie started to argue, but a voice in her head kept telling her she needed her friends. "All right. I'll wait here, but you and Saul have got to promise me you'll be careful, Leona. The roads are going to be slick."

Somehow Ruthie managed to get a pot of coffee brewing in the Bunn. She was about to pour herself a cup when she heard pounding on the diner window.

Etta May and Nola Gay's noses were plastered against the new glass. Apparently, Leona had summoned the troops.

"Key's under the mat," Ruthie shouted.

The twins let themselves in. Both women carried big baskets of canned goods, homegrown vegetables, and sandwiches.

Etta May lined up jars on the counter. "We thought you might be hungry, Ruthie."

"This is a diner," Ruthie said. "I've got plenty of food." Which was true for tonight because these two old women had selflessly helped rejuvenate her business so she could pay for the groceries Angus bought before he and Earl Dean left for the lake. "Just no stomach for eating alone."

"I told you, Sister," Nola Gay said to Etta May. "Good company is what our Ruthie needs."

"I could stand some company that's for sure." And Ruthie meant it. "And some prayers." And she meant that too.

Etta May smiled and thumped the metal ring sealing a jar of pickled okra. "Good thing because we didn't know what else to do but activate the prayer chain."

Nola Gay picked up her empty basket. "Just wanted you to know that we love Angus like he is our own."

These friends were good women. They'd managed to keep upbeat attitudes toward everyone, including her and her cranky ways. Life had cheated them out of husbands and children, but they'd not let their lost dreams turn them barn sour.

"Thank you, ladies. For everything." Ruthie raised the carafe. "Coffee?"

"Let me pour." Nola Gay set her basket on an empty booth. "Your hands are shaking worse than a butterfly in a strong wind."

Without argument, Ruthie turned the weight of her burden over to Nola Gay. She watched as the old woman filled three heavy mugs then joined her and Etta May at a table. Spoons clinked as they all silently stared out the window, watching the wind whip the Christmas parade banners against the light poles.

Roxie burst inside with the force of a woman determined not to let cancer slow her down. She wore a stocking cap pulled low over the thick mahogany waves Ruthie prayed cancer wouldn't steal from her. "I sent Tom to tell Howard to tell the search team that if they need anything, they have my number." She poured herself a cup of coffee, added her chair to the circle, then silently slipped in beside Ruthie.

To Ruthie's relief, no one tried to make small talk or tell her that Angus and Earl Dean would be just fine, or worst of all, try to convince her that she shouldn't blame herself.

The bell above the door tinkled again.

Leona bustled in and strode straight for Ruthie's open arms without even stopping to remove her coat and gloves. "I've been praying since the moment you called," she whispered in Ruthie's ear.

Ruthie held tight to Leona and her unshakable faith. "This is all my fault."

Leona pushed back, then took Ruthie's hands in hers. "Do not say that again, Ruthie Crouch."

"But it is." Ruthie blinked back tears. "If I'd divorced Earl Dean years ago, he would not have had a reason to turn up now. The diner would be mine . . . if I wasn't behind on my rent." She looked up. Her relief that she'd let the whole truth finally come tumbling out quickly turned to surprise that no one seemed shocked by her admission.

"Ruthie," Leona sank into the chair Roxie had added to the circle for her. "Sometimes the people we love the most are the hardest to like."

"I like Earl Dean fine, Leona," Ruthie admitted. "Always have." Releasing one truth had set in motion her ability to freely speak other truths. "Whatever he saw, or did, in that ugly war was a ball and chain he can't seem to slip."

"Ruthie." Leona took a deep breath, but it was the caution on her face that claimed Ruthie's full attention. "Saul wanted you and Earl Dean to be present when he shared what he's found on Earl Dean's military record."

Ruthie held up her hand. "I don't want to hear anything bad about my husband, Leona. That man has suffered enough." Ruthie glanced at the swollen fingers poking out from her cast. "And most of it at my hands."

"That's just it, Ruthie," Leona said. "Private Earl Dean Crouch is a decorated military hero." Leona pulled some official looking papers from her purse and placed them on the table. "See?"

"Well, I declare," Etta May craned her head trying to read the upside-down words. "A Purple Heart." She looked to Nola Gay. "I told you there was more to Earl Dean's story, Sister."

"A hero." Ruthie repeated, trying to take in a possibility she'd never considered. "How can that be?"

"He risked his life to rescue some soldiers from a burning chow hall that had taken a direct hit from a missile." Leona's words sounded garbled in Ruthie's head, but she managed to make out, "He was ordered to evacuate the area, but he refused to run away."

Ruthie shook her head. "If he had that kind of courage, how could he so easily run away from me?"

"Was it easy?" Leona laid a hand on Ruthie's cast. "That's something only Earl Dean can answer."

These women sitting around her table surely had as many questions as she, but they kindly kept their curiosity to themselves. The pounding in her ears was the judge's gavel of her own conscience declaring her guilty of judgmental and unforgiving ways.

Roxie made another pot of coffee, then cut one of the apple pies Earl Dean had made for the parade crowd everyone expected tomorrow. Roxie doled out respectable slices, but Ruthie couldn't stomach a bite. How many years had she wasted believing the worst of everyone?

Around midnight, Ruthie heard the rumble of engines. Several sets of headlights swept the booth where Etta May and Nola Gay dozed and Leona and Roxie poured over last-minute parade details.

"That's them, ain't it?" Ruthie managed to say despite the parched-mouth fear she'd been chewing on for hours. "I can't look."

"Stay here." Leona patted Ruthie's arm and slid from the booth. She went to the window. "They're home!" she shouted.

"Both of them?" Ruthie asked.

"I don't know." Leona flew to the door, the bell jangling as she thrust it open. "It's freezing out there. Hurry. Come inside, fellas," she told the men gathering on the sidewalk.

Heart pounding, Ruthie unlocked her wheelchair and rolled, as best she could with only one good arm, toward the door. "Angus!" she called. "Earl Dean!"

Howard Davis stepped into the diner. He had hold of the limp arm of a very wet but still alive old man draped over his shoulder.

"Earl Dean!" Ruthie's cry tore at her throat. "Where's my boy? I told you he couldn't swim."

"Ruthie—" Earl Dean's explanation was interrupted by Etta May.

"It's Angus." Etta May was elbowing Nola Gay awake. "Our boy's home."

David and Saul stepped into the diner with Angus, wet and exhausted, steadied between them.

"Angus!" Ruthie rolled past Earl Dean. "Come to MeMaw!"

"Sorry I let your truck slide off the bridge, but we were spinning before I knew it," slipped through her grandson's chattering teeth. "PePaw saved me." Her grandson lifted a large stringer of catfish. "And our mess of fish."

Chapter Nineteen

Ruthie

The aroma of fish frying woke Ruthie from a fitful dream. She reached for a tissue and dabbed the sweat from her face. No matter how tightly she closed her eyes, the image of Angus falling into the dark, cold waters of the creek had plagued her mind all night.

She rolled toward the small window, her good leg smacking into her clunky leg cast.

The cool, blue light of morning peeked around the sides of the drawn shade and brought her bolt upright. What had happened last night was no dream.

Angus *had* slipped under the creek's rushing waters. She would have lost her grandson if Earl Dean hadn't risked his own life to free his seatbelt and drag him to shore. Ruthie clutched at the pain in her chest and tried to steady her breathing. Courage in the face of danger was another point in Earl Dean's favor. A side of him Leona claimed his Purple Heart proved was true, but courage was a part of him she'd had a hard time believing because he'd acted so cowardly by leaving her.

Ruthie hauled herself to the edge of the bed. She reached for the pile of clothes she'd dropped on her wheelchair last night, too emotionally wrung out to do much more than slip into her gown. But she wasn't tired anymore. The clarity and strength that had carried her through these last forty years would carry her through what she had to do now.

She hurried and dressed in the makeshift bedroom Angus had made for her in the storage closet behind the diner grill.

Wrestling into her day dress wasn't nearly as hard as fastening the buttons with her casted arm. A quick glance in the small mirror hanging near the door told her that her hair was as tangled as her stomach. She jerked the comb through her thick gray strands, but the knots refused to be smoothed. As for the wrinkles on her face, anger and worry had carved them deep. Nothing to be done about the scars years of raging emotions had inflicted.

But she could do something to keep anger and worry from doing any more damage. She was not getting any younger and neither was Earl Dean. The conversation they should have had years ago could be put off no longer.

Ruthie rolled into the hall at the base of the stairs. From the apartment above, the deep breathing of the young man exhausted from his near-death experience drifted through the aroma of fried fish. Angus was alive and sleeping in the home she'd made for him. For those two miracles, she would be forever grateful. She intended to acknowledge Earl Dean's part in saving the boy's life. His heroic act had paid her back, in full, and she wanted to thank him.

To forgive him for coming home.

To forgive him for leaving.

To forgive him everything.

Ruthie turned her wheelchair toward the whistled tune coming from the diner's grill and spun herself toward redemption.

When she arrived in the dining room, she found Earl Dean shaking the fryer baskets. With his sleeves pushed to his elbows, an apron tied around his thin neck, and a Santa hat perched on his head, he seemed transformed from the sad-sack man who'd ventured inside the diner a few weeks ago.

Ruthie maneuvered her chair behind the counter. "Morning."

Earl Dean jumped with a start, grabbed a spatula, then wheeled in a defensive position. His eyes wide and terrified.

"Earl Dean," Ruthie said, doing her best to keep her voice calm and reassuring. "It's just me, Ruthie."

It took a few seconds for him to bring her into focus. "Ruthie?" Breathing hard, he lowered the spatula, embarrassment on his face. "Sorry. Didn't hear you coming."

"Didn't mean to set you off."

He pivoted away from her and lifted a basket of crispy catfish strips from the fryer. "It don't take much." His hands shook as he worked to move the fish to a serving tray.

The skittishness she'd noticed when he returned from the war was still there. He'd obviously learned to reel his agitation in faster, but she could see it lurking beneath the surface, coiled like a snake behind his smile.

She took one of the pieces of hot fish from the tray. As she blew on the crispy crust, a memory surfaced. A desperate Hail Mary she'd tried forty years ago to help Earl Dean adjust to life at home again. She'd packed him a lunch and sent him fishing. The later it got, the more she worried she'd done the wrong thing. But around midnight, he'd come back, happier than she'd seen him since he'd been discharged. They'd made love. They'd cuddled and giggled like newlyweds afterwards. She'd placed Earl Dean's hand upon her swollen belly, and he'd laughed when he felt baby Ruby kick. Later, while still wrapped in each other's arms, they'd told each other the worst was behind them.

Ruthie took a deep breath and held up the crispy fish nugget. "You used to say, 'Any day that starts with fried fish is a good day.' Remember?"

Earl continued rolling fish strips in his secret concoction of white corn meal and Cajun spices. "I do, Ruthie." He dropped the basket of breaded fish strips into the hot grease. The fingerlings sizzled. He turned and looked her in the eye, his hands still a little shaky. "Thought about coming back and fixing you a catfish breakfast every single time I fried one."

From the hurt on his face, the confession had been as hard for him to make as it had been for her to hear. "You eat a lot of fish, do you?" She bit into the fish. Perfect as she remembered.

He nodded. "Doctor said fish was good for my heart."

"Speaking of hearts. . ." Suddenly aware that the question she'd mulled all night could trigger Earl Dean's tendency to bolt, she let the phrase hang in the air. Crazy to think, but could she possibly need him to stay worse than she needed answers? She wheeled to the Bunn and helped herself to fresh coffee.

"Ruthie?" Earl Dean asked. "What do you want to know?"

Praying the strength she heard in his voice meant he was ready to face the past, she hooked the handle of her mug and said gently, "Why didn't you tell me about your Purple Heart?"

His lips clamped. Her need for explanations had cut the thin line of communication last night's celebration had opened. Any minute, he'd rip off his apron and be gone. But instead of running, he turned and shook the fryer basket. The hot grease roiled.

Earl Dean took a deep breath, then faced her. "When my transport plane landed back on US soil, people were still protesting the war. Our commander told what was left of my unit that it was best not to talk about what we'd seen or what we'd done."

"Your commander ain't here now." Ruthie filled another mug and held it out to him. "I deserve to hear the truth, and I want to hear it from you."

He took the cup. "That you do." His roughened fingers brushed hers and they both pulled back like they'd stuck their finger in a light socket.

"Well?" Ruthie said. "I ain't getting any younger."

In a few minutes, Earl Dean had the last basket of fish removed from the grease and they were sitting across from each other. Ruthie leaned forward on her elbows, as eager to hear his story as Earl Dean was reluctant to tell it.

Steam rose from the mug he clasped. "When you told me you were pregnant," his speech slowed as if he couldn't bear the shame of remembering. "I got scared. Felt so tied down I couldn't breathe."

"You weren't drafted into that war, were you?"

He shook his head slowly. "I went and signed up."

She hadn't let herself believe what she'd known all along. He'd gone to war to escape her. She had nothing to say to this.

But Earl Dean apparently had more to say because he took in a rattly breath and leaned toward her. "The moment I landed in Nam, I knew I'd exchanged one kind of confinement for a worse one." Earl Dean stirred his black coffee with the determination of a man trying to banish the dark demons. "Since I had cooking experience, I was assigned to work the chow hall." His spoon clinked against the mug. "I'd seen some of the fighting men carried back into camp on stretchers. Blown half to bits. I thought the chow hall sounded like a safe place to ride this out. So, I spent my days, peelin' tators and tellin' myself I wouldn't be a coward if I came back to Mt. Hope and settled down. Faced my fears. Took a stab at bein' the father I never had."

Ruthie had so many questions, but she could feel that with one wrong word, he'd be off faster than an alley cat. She made herself wait silently for the rest of the story.

He dared a quick glance at her, his eyes heavy with regret and a tiny spark of the steely determination she'd not seen in years. "I'd just finished the lunch shift and was heading to my bunker for a break and the pack of cigarettes you'd sent me." He swallowed hard, looked past her like he was looking into a scene from years ago. "I heard this terrible explosion. Turned around right as the chow hall burst into flames. Friends of mine were in that kitchen making lunch. I didn't even stop to think. I started running toward them." Earl Dean's lip quivered. "A rocket landed behind me. The blast threw me forward. By the time I woke up, the mess hall was nothing but a pile of smoldering debris." His voice faltered and he had to work to finish his story. "If I'd been able to stay on my feet, those boys wouldn't have died."

"You sure that's true, Earl Dean?"

"I got a piece of shrapnel in my leg." He tapped his spoon on the rim of the mug. "Those boys died, and I got the medal for bravery."

"Earl—" She started to reach for him.

"When I came home, it wasn't the town I couldn't stand. Or the thought of being a father." He clasped his hands into a fist. "It was never you I ran from, Ruthie."

"Then what?"

"It was the thought of everyone thinking I was a hero when I was nothing more than a coward hiding behind a cookstove."

"If you'd stayed here after you came back, we would have found you something else to do."

"Maybe, but at the time, well . . . I couldn't find myself. I was lost, you know? A walking, talking, breathing empty shell."

All those efforts she'd made years ago to pull him back had been like tossing coins into a dry well.

"For a long time," he said. "I could hear their voices. Calling to me. I'd run to save them, but before I could get to them, I'd fall. Every time." Tears swam in his eyes. "If I could have only stayed on my feet, Ruthie . . . I could have stayed here."

"Where did you go after you left?"

He shrugged. "Here and there at first. Then after a couple of hard years of panhandling, I finally landed a job at a ranch not far from here. I worked cattle and built fence. Dusty, hard work that kept me so tired that when I laid my head on the pillow at night, I didn't have the energy to remember Nam."

"Or me?" Fury rose up past his silence and spewed from Ruthie's tongue. "So, you've been livin' close by all this time?"

His *yes* was no more than a whisper. "I stayed at the ranch until that job petered out."

"Then what?"

"Moved on to the next ranch. And then another."

"For forty years?" Ruthie fought back her own tears. "You never thought of us, or coming home, for forty years?"

"I thought of you every day, Ruthie. One time, I even caught a bus and made it all the way to the diner door. When I peered through the window, I saw the diner full of customers and the cutest little redheaded girl sitting on the counter, sipping a root beer float, and making everyone laugh while you fried burgers."

"Why didn't you come in?"

"Still couldn't handle crowds," he said. "Besides, I could see that you'd become such a strong woman, you didn't need a man."

"I've never needed a man, Earl Dean." Anger propelled her so far forward she felt her chair tip. "I needed my husband and best friend."

A long pause spread between them.

When Ruthie couldn't stand the silence another second, she sank back into her seat and asked the question that had been burning inside her from the moment he'd shown up unannounced. "Why come back now?"

He did not hesitate. "To thank you."

"Thank me?" she asked, the surprise evident in her voice. "For what?"

"That day I got a glimpse of you boldly putting one foot in front of the other I'll admit, at first, your success made me feel even smaller. I hated myself for all the pain I'd caused you and all I'd missed with our little girl. But something about seeing your courage that day gave me the strength to fight my demons."

Ruthie felt the walls around her heart begin to crumble. "Have you won?" She held her breath, praying for his sake, not hers, that he had.

He shrugged. "One of the ranchers I worked for in Montana was a good Christian man. A veteran himself. He told me I'd never be free of my demons until I came back and made things right." Earl Dean looked her square in the eye. "Told you to your face that I'm sorry. Real sorry, Ruthie." Before she could say she could see his remorse, he said, "That good man gave me my final payment in cash and told me to use it to head back to Texas."

Ruthie's mind was reeling, trying to reconcile this difficult version of Earl Dean's life with the narrow perspective she'd clung to for the last forty years. "So, you caught a bus to Mt. Hope?"

He shook his head. "Walked."

"From Montana?"

"Needed time to build up the courage to step into your happy place." He lowered his head. "Came to the door twice and left twice because dredging up the past would be hard on you."

Ruthie let her mind drift back to those worn-out boots Earl Dean was wearing when he finally stepped through the diner door. There wasn't a shred of sole left on them after miles and miles of toting heavy burdens over hard pavement and bad weather. It was a miracle the man made it here at all. Maybe she hadn't physically walked hundreds of miles, but she knew the weight of carrying the world on your shoulders. She knew the tremendous effort it had required for Earl Dean to keep going.

The tower of anger inside of her cracked wide open. As the ugliness drained away, she felt warmth thick and as delicious as hot fudge begin to pump through her icy veins. "I'm glad you found the courage to come home, Earl Dean."

"You are?"

"I am." And she made sure he could tell from the smile on her face that she meant it.

"But I nearly got our grandson killed."

"You've given Angus something he's never had."

"A fishing lesson?"

"No, you old fool," she chuckled. "A father figure."

Earl Dean swiped at the tear running down his cheek. "I am sorry I've missed out on so much, Ruthie. And that's the truth of it."

A complete and unexpected feeling of forgiveness swept away any remaining shards of anger.

"I hate that for you too, Earl Dean."

It was true her life had been hard, but it had also been good in so many ways. She'd experienced so many shared laughs around the tables in this very room, she could hear the echoes still. People came to her diner hungry. They left with their bellies full and their hearts happy.

"Despite all my struggles, Earl Dean, the Lord's blessed me with lots of friends and family."

"I can see he has. There's not a rotten apple in the bunch."

"Well, there's Howard Davis," Ruthie said. "But underneath Howard's crusty exterior, there's a man who'll give me a fair deal when I go to trade in my wrecked F150."

They both chuckled.

"If I had stuck around, maybe all these fine folks would have been my friends too."

"They'll be your friends now."

"Don't they blame me for what happened with Ruby?"

"Ain't a one in the bunch who hasn't made their fair share of mistakes." Ruthie took a sip of coffee then asked, "Angus tell you about his mother?"

Earl Dean nodded. "He says she loved him big."

"Ruby did everything big, including loving that boy," Ruthie said. "Our girl grew up surrounded by diner regulars—a coffee klatch of old men who made over her and called her sweetie and special." Ruthie let her eyes drift to the booth where the group used to sit. "I wanted to believe their kindness toward her was enough to make up for the lack of a father, but I knew it wasn't. So, I indulged her. Thought that I could smother the wanderlust out of her. I was so determined she was not going to be anything like *you* that I spoiled her rotten. But everything I gave her only fed her desire for more. She started to believe the world was her oyster and somewhere out there was the pearl that would make her happy." Ruthie dabbed a tear with a napkin. "In the end, I don't think she went in search of you. I think she left to get away from me."

"Hate me, Ruthie," he said. "Not yourself."

"Oh, make no mistake, I've spent these past years hating you plenty," Ruthie admitted. "But I don't hate you anymore, Earl Dean."

His shoulders lifted a little. "I'm so very sorry for my part in our daughter's struggles."

"I carried the shame of my part in her struggles a good long while," Ruthie admitted. "But I feel the Lord gave me a second chance do a better job loving a kid when he sent me Angus."

"He's a good boy, that one."

"The best of both of us."

"That's a kindness," he said. "Another kindness I don't deserve."

A different ending to their stories began to form in her head.

"Earl Dean," she said, noting that his name no longer scalded her tongue, "The things you and I have done, or have failed to do, are in the past." She took a risk and reached for his hand. She wanted to hold it tight, but she'd learned love was a fickle thing. Easily smothered and snuffed out. She rested her fingers lightly against his roughened knuckles. "If you want a permanent home, you've got one here."

Chapter Twenty

Ruthie

Parade day morning, Earl Dean patted the belly pillow Ruthie had helped him tuck inside his red Santa suit. "Wish I could give you back even a tiny bit of the peace you've given me, Ruthie."

"We're square." She slipped her apron over her head. "Ready?"

His hands were shaking, a sure sign he was still worried about all the loud noises and crowd. "Might need a smoke."

"You can do this, Earl Dean. I've seen the way you light up the faces of the kids stopping by to see Santa over at Brewer's."

"But that's just a few folks at a time."

She no longer wished to impose her expectations on him. "If playing Santa for the parade is too much pressure, Angus can slip on the suit."

Earl Dean shook his head. "I've been shirking responsibilities long enough. The town's counting on me." He glanced around the diner. "You got a nice place here, Ruthie."

"Well, this makeover is thanks to Leona Levy, Angus Freestone, and you."

"No, I meant it's a warm, welcoming place to be," he said. "Folks like coming in here, getting a bite to eat, and feeling like someone cares. And you alone are responsible for that, Ruthie."

"The Koffee Kup has been good to me, but it won't be for much longer." She swallowed hard and told him her secret. "I'm behind on the rent."

Earl Dean shrugged like she'd just said they were out of milk, and he thought it was no big deal. "Angus might have mentioned your financial situation while we were fishing."

"He knows?"

"That boy's not like me. He'd never leave you in a lurch." Earl Dean stroked his beard like a man still struggling to forgive himself. "Sooner we get this show on the road, sooner you'll have some money in your cash drawer." He flipped the front door lock.

The council streamed in, jabbering excited good mornings to Santa and then to her. Leona stopped at Ruthie's wheelchair and asked after Angus.

"Letting the exhausted boy sleep in a bit," Ruthie said. "But he'll be down to help in a split jiffy once he hears all this racket."

Leona laughed. "He's a good boy, Ruthie."

"Don't I know it."

"We'll try to keep our excitement to a low roar." Leona herded her little parade-day team toward the back two tables Earl Dean had pulled together in advance of this planned meeting. "Something sure smells good."

“Earl Dean’s been up frying fish since four this morning.” Ruthie couldn’t help but marvel at the pride in her voice. “Behave yourselves, and I’ll give y’all a little pre-parade taste.”

Ruthie and Earl Dean worked together to keep the coffee cups filled as the council went over the last-minute details.

Etta May and Nola Gay needed a couple of safety pins to hold their elf costumes in place. Howard worried that the overcast sky threatened to dump more ice on Main Street. Everyone thanked Earl Dean for agreeing to play the part of Santa. Leona asked Roxie again if she was sure she was up to driving a combine down the middle of Main Street.

“Hell’s bells, Leona.” Roxie pulled the knitted Santa cap over the beautiful hair Ruthie prayed she’d get to keep. “I’m not going to miss a chance to show off the latest Story sisters’ venture.”

“Venture?” Leona asked.

Etta May held up a ball of red yarn. “We’re knitting Santa hats to sell.”

Everyone told Roxie that her new hat looked great, and the beaming Story sisters pulled out knitted hats for everyone, including one for Angus.

“Well, then,” Leona said patting her Santa hat into place. “Looks like everything is under control.” She smiled at her little band of ready and willing participants. “Break a leg everyone.” Then she looked at Ruthie and promptly took it back. “You know what I mean.”

Everyone laughed, including Ruthie. Earl Dean held out a tray of crispy catfish and everyone grabbed a hot piece.

“Oh, my,” Leona said, savoring the crunchy nugget. “Earl Dean, you are a multi-talented Santa.” Everyone agreed, then one by one they headed out into the cold to man their parade stations.

Ruthie gave Earl Dean a proud nod and his face blushed as red as his hat.

"Earl Dean." Roxie stopped at the door. "Charlie thought Santa's arrival deserved flashing lights and a siren, so he put the hitch on his ambulance. He'll be pulling your Santa trailer."

Ruthie saw terror flash in Earl Dean's eyes. All the loud noises and flashing lights might be asking too much of a man traumatized by war. "Roxie, shouldn't Charlie keep his ambulance free in case there's a medical emergency?"

"Today, everyone stays healthy. Right, Earl Dean?" Roxie blew him a kiss.

"Yes ma'am." Earl Dean stood ramrod straight, eyes so wide Ruthie could see the conflict between civic duty and panic swirling in them. "Everyone."

"Charlie is parked behind my store." Roxie tugged on her gloves. "Come with me, and I'll get you settled on your hay bales before I fire up the John Deere."

Earl Dean nodded, but he didn't move. His hands were trembling, and Ruthie detected a slight sway in his stance.

Ruthie wheeled her chair next to Earl Dean. "Roxie, I think Earl Dean needs a bite to eat to level out his blood sugar. I'll have Angus take him to his trailer right before the parade starts. No point in him sitting out in the cold and catching a chill."

Roxie looked from Ruthie to Earl Dean. "Life is short. Don't let fear keep you from claiming every scrap of happiness." If she could tell Santa was feeling jumpy, she was too fine a person to mention it.

Once Roxie was gone, Ruthie turned to Earl Dean. "You don't have to do this."

He sucked in a deep breath. "For once, I'm going to keep a promise." He picked up his backpack. "I can find the hay trailer." On his way out the diner door, he turned and said over his shoulder, "You've got this, Ruthie. You always have."

She watched Earl Dean trudge across the street, responsibility heavy as the pack on his back. As the far-too-skinny Santa disappeared around the corner of the building, she had to fight the urge to wheel out after him to keep him from disappearing forever.

Angus laid his hand on her shoulder. "MeMaw?"

"You're up early."

"Didn't want to miss our Santa coming to town."

If she'd learned anything these last two weeks, it was that the only person she could change was herself. Earl Dean's change was up to him and God. "It's going to be something, that's for sure."

"I could play Santa if the attention is too much for PePaw."

She was glad to hear Angus calling his grandfather by the term of endearment again, but she couldn't help but worry about how she would fix her grandson's broken heart if Earl Dean's demons won and he disappeared. "I'm afraid this is something your PePaw needs to do on his own."

For once, Angus didn't argue. He helped Ruthie bundle up in a coat and the red hat knitted by the Storys, and then he set a pan of warm catfish fingerlings in her lap. "Maybe we should cut them into smaller pieces, MeMaw."

"We don't do smaller pieces at this diner, Angus *Dean* Freestone."

Angus smiled when he heard how proudly she said his middle name. "Yes, ma'am." He donned his own new red stocking cap then wheeled her out into the biting wind.

Barricades blocked Main Street at each end. No cars had been allowed to park on either side of the street, but the sidewalks swarmed with excited folks. Early birds had placed their lawn chairs near the curb. Latecomers stood three-deep behind them. Everyone huddled beneath blankets and sipped hot drinks from insulated thermoses.

"It's been years since I've seen a crowd like this on Main Street." Ruthie removed the foil covering from the pan. The delicious aroma of fried fish immediately turned heads. Within seconds, she'd given away her samples. Angus hurried inside, refilled the pan, and Ruthie emptied this batch almost as quickly as she'd emptied the first.

"Angus," Ruthie said, so energized she no longer felt the cold. "Do we have a reservation book?"

"We sure do." Angus ducked inside the diner and returned with a notebook. Within minutes, they were booked solid until three o'clock.

By the time the bells chimed on the Mt. Hope Community Church steeple, the rodeo queen was in the lead parade position on her prancing horse. The beautiful girl with long black curls and a white cowboy hat waved to the crowd, clicked the reins of her sleek chestnut stallion, and started down Main Street.

People cheered as the parade queen smiled and threw candy. Ten horses, ridden by the members of the 4-H riding club, followed her lead. The riders were trailed by two fathers pulling rolling trash cans and the official pooper-scooper shovels. Next came the high school marching band, drums beating and trumpets blaring at a safe and respectful distance behind the horses.

Ivan stopped in front of Ruthie. "Let's give Leona something special for the front page. Smile." He snapped a picture of Ruthie and Angus with the blinking Koffee Kup sign in the background. "I hear the Storys' lawn mowers. Gotta go." His eyes twinkling for the first time since he'd lost his Hathleen, Ivan spun from Ruthie and began to elbow his way through the crowd for a good shot of the Story twins.

"You see that smile on Ivan's face, MeMaw?" Angus asked.

"I sure did."

"Hope that means he's sticking around," Angus said. "I could learn so much from him."

"What are you talking about?"

Angus squatted in front of her. "I've been helping out at the paper and . . ."

"And you love it."

"I do, but I could never leave you, MeMaw." Angus patted her knee. "After the parade stuff settles down, I'm going to tell Mrs. L that I'm all yours again."

Before she could straighten out his undying allegiance to her, the loud roar of the riding lawn mowers driven by Etta May and Nola Gay dressed as matching elves made talking this fool notion through impossible. The old Story twins waved to the cheering crowd as they steered their identical small tractors down the center of Main. When they reached the stretch of street in front of the diner, they ramped up their show and cut a few figure eights. The crowd went wild. If the sisters hadn't nearly crashed into each other, those two old women might never have moved on.

Suddenly, the sidewalk began to vibrate. Ruthie craned her neck. An oversized green John Deere harvester rumbled down the street. Behind the steering wheel, Ruthie could see Roxie's red stocking cap and her huge smile. A gigantic BREWER'S AUTO & TRACTOR PARTS banner flapped from the fifty-foot-wide header that nearly swept those standing too close to the street from their feet.

"One stop tractor and auto parts," Roxie shouted through a megaphone while she took her hands from the wheel just long enough to point toward her store.

In the wake of diesel fumes, kids riding bikes and trikes decorated with Christmas streamers cycled past. Parents snapped pictures of their children while Ivan took pictures of parents taking pictures.

This overload of cuteness was followed by "Hark! The Herald Angels Sing" blaring from the state-of-the-art sound system of a late-model black F150. From the open window of the pickup's driver's seat, Howard tossed candy in hopes of drawing the crowd's attention toward the nativity float built by Mt. Hope Community Church. Pastor David and the entire Harper family waved from the beautifully constructed stable tableau. To Ruthie's relief, the only live animal near the plastic Jesus was a small puppy held by the oldest of the young pastor's children.

Finally, the moment everyone had been waiting for was announced by the piercing wail of Charlie's ambulance. Red and blue lights flashed.

Cheering children shoved their way to the curb shouting, "It's Santa!"

Ruthie's heart lurched. She sent up a silent prayer for Earl Dean's nerves.

The ambulance idled along, pulling a hay-covered flatbed trailer. Sitting on the top bale that had been decorated with cardboard painted to look like a red sleigh was . . . Santa . . . and he was looking for someone . . . he was looking for her.

Ruthie waved. "Merry Christmas, Santa."

When Earl Dean spotted her, he brought his finger to his nose and winked. Looking like he'd been Santa his whole life, he went back to smiling and waving at the children.

Tears trickled down Ruthie's cheeks. He'd done it. He'd conquered the voices in his head. He'd stayed when he'd wanted to go.

Children scampered past Ruthie, racing out to the street to snatch up the candy Earl Dean tossed their way.

As soon as the trailer with Santa rounded the corner, the parade was over. But Ruthie could feel something new stirring in the air.

Angus wheeled her inside the diner. Before she had time to warm up, the diner began to hum with business. From her wheelchair, Ruthie worked the welcome podium. Angus rushed from one end of the grill to the other. They were at capacity and had folks lined up down the block by the time Earl Dean finished his Santa run and managed to sneak in the diner's back door, still dressed in his red suit.

Earl Dean cheeks were cherry, flushed with joy. He flung an apron over his head, then took the spatula from his grandson. "That was something else."

Angus smiled big. "*You* were something else, PePaw." They hugged, then got to work filling orders.

Etta May and Nola Gay, still dressed as elves, burst through the diner door. "What can we do?" Etta May panted.

"We need some tables bussed," Ruthie said, glad for the extra help.

Leona bustled in, her face aglow at her Christmas parade success. "Put me to work, Ruthie."

Without hesitation, Ruthie turned over the welcome station. "You get people seated. I'll take orders."

It was close to three o'clock in the afternoon before the last customer had been served. Etta May and Nola Gay gathered the leftover pickles and called it a day. Leona and Saul cleared the last of the tables. Before they said their goodbyes, Leona thanked Earl Dean again for doing such a good job as Santa.

Earl Dean put down his spatula. "It's me who should be thanking you." He rubbed the back of his neck. "Felt good to do something for someone else."

Ruthie opened the cash drawer and drew out a wad of cash. "Leona, I know this won't pay all of Roxie's medical bills, but maybe it will give her some peace of mind while she's going through her treatments."

Leona pushed the money back to her. "You've got your own rent to pay, Ruthie."

Ruthie let her gaze slide around the diner. She loved these freshly painted, grease-splattered walls, the wobbly metal tables, the black and white checkered floor, and especially the mammoth-sized grill. The Lord had provided this refuge when she didn't know how she would provide for her family. This diner had been good to her, and she'd loved every minute of running this business. But the same inner voice that had pressed her to let go of her anger against Earl Dean was now telling her it was time to let go of what she believed to be her only security. It was time to step out in faith. To see what the Lord had in store for her future.

Ruthie shook her head and shoved the money toward Leona. "That's what friends are for, right?"

Leona studied her, with a grin that said the depth of the friendship that had grown between them mattered as much to her as it did to Ruthie. "I couldn't have said it better myself." Leona slid the money into her purse then kissed Ruthie's cheek. "You're an admirable woman, Ruthie Crouch. Everyone in this town is blessed to call you friend."

Saul took his wife by the elbow. "It's starting to rain again. We'd better get home before the bridge on our road ices over."

"Maybe we'll get those signs posted one day." Leona tugged on her gloves. "Right, Ruthie?"

"Maybe if I send the county the bill for my new truck that will push them along," Ruthie agreed.

Leona kissed Ruthie's cheek. "You're a peach, Ruthie Crouch."

Ruthie said a prayer for the safety of the happy couple as they climbed into Leona's SUV. God had given Leona Harper a second chance she never saw coming when he'd sent Saul Levy her way. God had given Mt. Hope a second chance. That same God could give her a second chance at happiness.

Quiet fell over the diner.

At the metallic sound of a quarter falling through the slot in the jukebox, Ruthie grinned. Angus often put on a lively tune while he cleaned up, so she kept her eyes on the Levys' receding taillights . . . until Bing Crosby began to croon, "I'll Be Home for Christmas."

Ruthie froze, her hand still on the empty cash drawer. How did Angus know that she and Earl Dean had danced to this song the night before he'd shipped out? As he'd twirled her around the diner that long ago night, Earl Dean had promised he'd come back. She'd thought about having the song removed from the selections, but never could bring herself to do it.

Ruthie spun her chair around slowly, her heart beating to the rhythm of the song.

Earl Dean stood at the jukebox. His outstretched fingers motioned her forward beneath the white fur of his red sleeve. "Can you still cut a rug?"

"She can," Angus shouted from the grill. "Best dancer I ever saw."

Earl Dean took a step toward her wheelchair. "Dance with me, Ruthie."

"Don't be ridiculous." She pointed at the cast on her leg. "I'm in no shape to dance."

"I didn't think I was in any shape to play Santa Claus." He wiggled his fingers again. "Just one spin around the floor."

"Earl Dean Crouch," she muttered. "You are the most aggravating man I've ever—"

"Come on, MeMaw." Angus was at her side and lifting her from her chair before she could finish her protest.

She looked at the two men God had sent her way. Both had been as lost as she, without a scrap of hope between any of them. How could she turn down the shot the Lord had given her to find happiness.

She held out her good hand. "Let's see if you've still got Bing Crosby moves, old man."

Earl Dean stepped forward. "Hope it's like riding a bike."

She laughingly toppled into his arms.

He held her upright, supported in the crook of his arm. The sound of Angus moving chairs and tables vaguely registered, but all Ruthie could think about was how wonderful it felt to be in the arms of the man she loved.

Slowly, Earl Dean began to sway. And just like riding a bike, her body began to follow his.

He pulled her close. "This is the life you deserved, Ruthie."

As the song's promise of coming home played on, Ruthie realized that no matter what happened between her and Earl Dean, the person she'd missed the most all these years was herself. The woman who used to love dancing, and laughing, and believing she had a purpose in this world. A woman so content with herself, she didn't need a man to make her happy.

Forgiving him completely was the path back to that woman.

She whispered in his ear. "I got better than I deserve, Earl Dean." She cupped his face between her good hand and her casted one. "And by God's grace, so will you."

He held her tight, like he wanted to believe a second chance was possible. But as they began to dance, she could feel him slipping away again, feel the goodbye in the way he moved his Santa boots toward the door. If, like Santa, he was only going to be here for one night, then she was going to enjoy this magical moment.

Chapter Twenty-One

Ruthie

It wasn't until after the menus were wiped down and the silverware bundles were rolled for the expected breakfast crowd that Ruthie noticed Earl Dean was no longer whistling behind the counter.

"Angus, you seen your PePaw?"

Her grandson stopped scraping hamburger grease into the trap, worry on his face. "Heard the screen door slam a while back."

Alarm squeezed her chest. "No," she whispered.

"No need to worry." Angus held up a napkin with something written on it. "Says he needed a smoke."

"Take me to the alley. Now!"

Ruthie's wheelchair bounced down the slick backdoor ramp. Her gaze frantically searched the cobblestones.

Nothing.

Not even a set of footprints in the snow.

"PePaw?" her grandson called. "PePaw!"

Ruthie reached for the flailing arm of her grandson. "He's gone, Angus."

"No." He backed away from her. "PePaw was settling in. He liked cooking. He..." Tears trickled down her grandson's ruddy cheeks.

She rolled toward him. "If leaving is what's best for him, then—"

"Hey," Earl Dean had strolled around the corner, surprise on his face. "What are you two doing out here in the cold?"

He'd stayed.

Joy. Relief. Love flooded Ruthie's soul. "Looking for you," she managed to say.

Earl Dean held up his backpack. "Left this on the Santa trailer. Forgot all about it until I went to get the present I have for you two." He looked at their open mouths. "What's the matter?"

Ruthie's relieved breath puffed little white clouds into the cold. "I thought—"

"You thought I'd hightailed it out of here again?"

"Yes."

"Can't blame you for that, but I want you to know I intend to earn your trust." Earl Dean lowered his eyes. "Because if your offer's still good, I'd like to stay."

"It's still good," Ruthie said.

Earl Dean lifted his head and smiled a big toothy grin. "Whether or not that was going to be your answer, I want you to have this little gift." Earl

Dean unzipped his backpack, reached inside, and pulled out a clear gallon bag. "Merry Christmas." He handed Ruthie the bag. "Sorry I didn't have time to wrap it with a bow."

By the light above the back door, she could see hundred-dollar bills. Lots of them "Did you rob a liquor store?"

"Saved every dime I could," Earl Dean said proudly. "I'm hopin' it'll be enough to pay off your rent debt and restock your pantry."

Tears warmed Ruthie's cheeks. "*Our* pantry."

"*Our* pantry," Earl Dean agreed, then leaned down and kissed her square on the mouth.

As his snowy white whiskers wrapped her lips, Ruthie felt all the warmth return to her heart. When Earl Dean finally pulled away, she smiled then turned to her grandson. "Angus, you can go on now. Take that journalism job Leona's offering. Make your mark on the world. Me and your *PePaw* are going to be just fine."

Snow began to fall, and Angus let out a loud, "This is going to be the best Christmas ever!"

Ruthie stretched out the swollen fingers poking from her cast. A tiny flake landed on her fingertip. She studied its intricate design. Another snowflake drifted down and landed next to it. And then another.

They were the same thing, these three snowflakes. Water transformed into snow. And yet they were so very different.

Unique. Beautiful. Perfect.

Instead of squeezing the flakes tight, she blew them free.

CHAPTER TWENTY-TWO

Leona

The delicious aroma of glazed ham permeated the parsonage. Christmas carols played through the new sound system David and Amy had installed. Leona stood at the sink washing the breakfast dishes as she looked out at the steepled building of Mt. Hope Community Church.

Memories of all the years she'd spent in this house worrying about how to achieve perfection in the Lord's house swirled before her like the curled leaves cartwheeling across the snow-dusted parking lot.

So much had happened since she'd arrived at this parsonage and bound herself in the lie that achieving perfection in her house somehow equaled perfection in the Lord's house. Fortunately, the Lord had freed her of this impossible burden. Unfortunately for her, her redemption had come through tragedy.

J.D.

Every time she returned to this house, she half expected her first husband to step out of his little office, Bible in hand, and ask her what's for supper. J.D., ever the eternal optimist, would not be surprised to learn that the pastoral work he'd done in this small west Texas town had accomplished more than the revitalization of a dying, little congregation. J.D. Harper's work had changed her. Freed her from the bondage of constantly striving for perfection.

"Thank you, J.D." Leona whispered as she slid her hands beneath the suds. "Thank you, Lord."

"Sure smells good in here, Momma." David reached around her and added his empty coffee cup to the growing pile of dirty pots and pans.

She dunked the cup in the water. "You were supposed to be helping your sister set the table for Christmas dinner."

"Maddie gave me a pass so I could put a few finishing touches on my sermon."

She looked up at the fine young man towering over her. "Your father would be so proud of you."

David grinned. "And you."

She chuckled. "He'd say, Leona, I'm glad to see you finally wearing those red shoes to church whenever you want."

David followed her gaze toward the church building. "I know the Lord's set you on a different path, but it sure seems like old times whenever you're here."

She rinsed the cup and set it in the drying rack. "It's been a good Christmas so far, hasn't it? Reminds me of so many of the Christmas mornings our family spent under this roof."

David nodded. "Every room in this house rings with Dad's laughter and your wisdom, Momma."

"I hope you can forgive our mistakes."

"Been too busy making my own mistakes to dwell on your miniscule infractions."

Leona dragged her fingers through the soap bubbles. "The Christmas Eve service was perfect."

"Come on, admit it," David teased. "You missed the pot brownies."

"I don't know, Angus laid out quite a spread last night."

"Without a single brownie in sight."

"Do you think Maxine was secretly disappointed?"

They couldn't contain the laughter.

"Hey, you two," Maddie said, a crystal water goblet in each hand. "I could use a little help keeping these wild and crazy kids clean until we leave for church."

After the Christmas Eve service, the entire family had gifted Leona with a surprise spend- the-night-at-the-parsonage party. Saul had helped her make kids' pallets on the floor, David had stirred up hot chocolate, and Maddie had helped the kids put out cookies for Santa. Watching the kids wake in the predawn hours to discover piles of presents under the tree had been glorious.

She smiled at her two grown children. They'd turned out perfect, despite her imperfect parenting. "We have been blessed under this roof, haven't we?"

"More than we could have asked or imagined," David said.

“I can’t thank my amazing family enough for helping to make this day special for everyone who worked so hard on the parade.”

“Hey, the credit for Mt. Hope’s current upturn belongs to you.” The doorbell rang. David raised one brow. “You know that’s the Story sisters, right?”

Leona dried her hands. “There are some things about living in this house I do not miss.”

The three of them shared another laugh, a hug, and their secret commitment to the Harper family doing whatever it took to keep hope alive, come what may.

Ten minutes later, the Story sisters, accompanied by the entire Harper family, crossed the parking lot between the parsonage and the church. In the foyer, Leona and Saul helped the old twins hang their coats on the same hook.

“Come on, Sister.” Nola Gay stuck out her arm. “Let’s get our seats.”

“You’re right, Sister.” Etta May threaded her arm through Nola Gay’s. “Attendance has increased so much we’ll have to hurry before someone claims our pew.”

From the back of the sanctuary, Leona let her gaze walk down the old carpet and skim the scuffed pews as if seeing the sacred place for the first time.

Up front, two Christmas trees wrapped in tiny white lights flanked the music-stand pulpit. David, a firm believer in removing as many barriers as possible between the pastor and his congregation, had no problem sacrificing his father’s large wooden pulpit for the sake of Ruthie’s diner renovation. "Harder to fall from a pedestal if you don't have one," he'd said.

Above the music stand, rays of sunlight framed the cross in the center of the stained-glass window. The wide garnet path twisting through mounds of multi-colored glass rocks became pinpoint small at the foot of the cross. For some reason, the image of a difficult road reminded her of the guilt trips J.D. used to tease her about. How easily she could have relieved herself of so much concern over what others thought of her if only she'd kept her eyes on the cross.

Saul slid his hand into hers. "Ready?" he whispered.

"Absolutely," she smiled.

As they made their way to the second pew from the front, she noticed Tom and Roxie sitting beside Howard and Maxine. The two couples had become inseparable since working together on the Christmas parade. Howard had started ordering all his truck parts from Roxie and Roxie had bought a used F150 from Howard. While radiation treatments had stolen Roxie's appetite and thinned her face, her battle with cancer had not diminished her smile or her insistence on coming today to hear David preach.

"Hell's bells, Leona," she'd said when Leona invited her to dinner on Christmas day, "Wild horses couldn't keep me away."

Behind the Davises and the Brewers, Modyne and her husband were waiting to squeeze in next to the Story sisters.

Leona stopped and took Modyne by the elbow. "Any word from Ivan?"

"Afraid not." Modyne noticed the slump in Leona's shoulders and quickly added, "You did your best to help him deal with his grief, Leona."

Modyne was not one to hand out compliments. And as much as Leona wanted to take comfort in Modyne's statement, she really didn't know if she'd helped the man who'd taught her so much. Some days she wanted to pinch herself because she was so happy running the newspaper. Other days she wanted to kick herself for relieving Ivan of his purpose.

"You'll let me know if he calls, right?"

Modyne patted her hand. "You know I will."

"Of that, I have no doubt."

The woman who used to scare her to death had stepped it up on so many levels since Leona took over the newspaper. They weren't just co-reporters they were a team. Subscriptions had more than tripled since Modyne and Angus built the *Messenger* a digital presence.

Speaking of Angus . . . Leona's gaze jumped the aisle.

Ruthie, Angus, and Earl Dean waved their greetings. Earl Dean's face had filled out a little, but it was the smiles on the faces of Ruthie and Angus that warmed her heart. A second chance was a gift she fully understood.

Saul and Leona seated themselves on the pew right behind David, who sat like a man who'd found where he belonged on Pastor's Row. Her grandkids scrambled to plant themselves either on her lap or Saul's. Maddie and Amy took the sentinel positions at each end of the pew.

Wilma Wilkerson transitioned from soft organ music to a rousing prelude when Parker took to the podium. Before Leona had time to secretly thank the Lord for all his blessings, the little sanctuary of Mt. Hope Community Church filled with praise.

After the service, people came through the parsonage door, their arms loaded with delicious contributions for the evening meal. The afternoon was spent playing games, telling tall tales, and devouring snacks.

Leona delayed the meal so long; the ham gravy had congealed. Finally, she had to concede that Ivan was not coming back to town.

“Let’s eat,” she announced as cheerfully as she could.

As David carved the huge ham, Leona let her gaze skip over Ivan’s empty place setting and began to take an inventory of her blessings.

Saul.

David and Amy.

Maddie and Parker.

Mother and Cotton.

Tom and Roxie.

Howard and Maxine.

Modyne and her husband.

The Story sisters.

Ruthie, Earl Dean, and Angus.

To an outsider, it might appear that she had nothing in common with these people. Each of them so different than she.

Yet, these people were family.

Her family.

Bound by their love for each other, this town, and most importantly, their love of God.

She reached under the table and squeezed Saul's hand. She didn't have to exchange eye contact with him to see if he understood that she was holding back tears. He knew what it meant for her to have everyone she loved gathered around the table in the home that had changed her life.

Night was falling. The dishwasher hummed as Leona stood at the sink peering into the growing darkness. The day had been filled with so much laughter, and yet her heart felt heavy.

Saul came up behind her and slid his arms around her waist. "Weather's getting bad. Folks are loading up to leave."

"Okay," she sighed. "I'm almost done here."

"He'll come home," Saul said, reading her mind.

"What if he doesn't?"

"Then you'll keep doing what you do best, and the newspaper Ivan's family started will remain a viable legacy."

"Hey, Momma," Maddie called from the living room. "You might want to come see this."

Leona and Saul hurried to investigate the commotion. She burst into the living room and found Ivan Tucker stomping snow from his boots on the entry tile.

"Ivan!" she shouted and ran to hug him. "You're back."

"Of course, I'm back." He pulled his camera from the bag slung over his shoulder. "I've got pictures to take and news to report." He turned his camera so she could see the digital screen. "Front page stuff right here."

Leona took the camera. Headlights shone on a reflective traffic sign nailed to a pole.

BRIDGES ICE IN WINTER

"Where did you get this?"

"Got a tip from one of the county commissioners." Ivan smiled. "They're going up on every bridge in the county." He took the camera from her and passed it to Saul. "You did it, Leona! That article you wrote about Angus spinning out finally loosened the strings on the county's checkbook."

"*We* did it, Ivan," Leona said. "Your pictures did it."

"Well," Ivan said. "What do you say?"

"I say that no one in this town is done." Leona turned to the friends and family gathered around her. "We're just getting started!"

Keep Reading

Aren't the people of Mt. Hope fun? If you've just discovered this series via **SANTA SHOES**, you'll be happy to know that you can get your hands on the first FOUR books in the series.

Don't worry. You can catch up.

Start with WALKING SHOES.

Thanks for joining the Harper family on this holiday leg of their Mt. Hope Southern Adventure.

Because you enjoyed **SANTA SHOES**, I'd appreciate it if you could leave a review. Your reviews and shares on social media make such a big difference when it comes to spreading the word about these stories.

I invite you to take a moment and sign up for my **Reader's Club**. As a member, you'll be the first to know of new releases, plus you'll get your FREE copy of the first ACT of my audio performance of this story. Sign up @ **www.lynnegentry.com** and start collecting all three audio acts.

INTRODUCING MY NEW SOUTHERN ADVENTURES SERIES

Since you loved the folks in Mt. Hope, you'll want to grab the first book in my newest **WOMEN OF FOSSIL RIDGE** series and slip away to the beautiful Texas Hill Country. These books explore the real-life struggles families face as parents age. The Slocum women are tough, funny, and stubborn. You'll laugh, cry, and root for everyone in this emotionally packed, inter-generational tale.

Twenty-five years ago, the Slocum women buried their mother-daughter relationship in the Frio River and went their separate ways. Sara and Charlotte pretend their weekly long-distance calls fulfill the extent of their obligation to each other until another lapse in Sara's judgment causes her to break her hip.

Now Charlotte must drop everything and fly to Texas. Charlotte's aging mother needs long-term care. While Sara struggles to regain her independence, Charlotte grapples with the impossible task of juggling her slightly demented mother, a high-pressure job, and a rebellious teenage daughter.

But unless these two women can release the fossilized secret sandwiched between them, the next generation will never fly.

The **WOMEN OF FOSSIL RIDGE** series is a touching addition to the small town, generational series of favorite authors like Ann B. Ross, Jan Karon, and Beth Hoffman.

Sneak Peek of FLYING FOSSILS:

Chapter 1

Sara: An Independent Mother

As usual, you're being overly dramatic, Charlotte Ann." I hug the phone receiver between my ear and shoulder, stretch the cord across the kitchen, then snag a butcher knife from the wooden block. "Putting a few dents in a lawnmower is hardly a reason for me to give up my ranch."

"Mother, you totaled a two-thousand-dollar *riding* mower!" My daughter's anger crackles on the line. "What if you'd been hurt?"

Contrary to Charlotte's insinuations, I'm not some fragile, rusty weathervane easily spun by the changing winds that sweep through these Texas Hill Country valleys. As per the invariant order of things, my feet have become deeply rooted in the rocky soil. I'm attached to this land tighter than the fossils that cling to the banks of the Frio River.

For forty-two years, I've been the mother. Charlotte the child. Simple laws govern our parent-child relationship. I'll admit, there are rules that allow for an orderly transition of power, if that sad time should ever come. But, I'll not be pushed into speeding things along simply because it suits Charlotte.

Trading roles with my daughter now would be like winter unexpectedly giving way to fall. Buds waiting to bloom would shrivel and die. There'd be no crops to harvest. Birds would never head north. Nothing would ever be right again. I know, because twenty-three years ago I was forced to go against the expected order of life. It was a tragedy that has ruined everything.

"Mother, did you hear me?" Somewhere in Charlotte's aggravation, I hear the little girl I used to know, the one who sat beside me on the piano bench...frustrated that she was having difficulty mastering Twinkle, Twinkle Little Star...worried that she never would.

I shift the receiver and whack a Bartlett pear into tiny pieces. "Don't worry, I'll pay you back."

"You know this is not about the money!" Charlotte barks.

"Then why did you bring it up?" I ignore my daughter's huge sigh and slide a piece of fruit through the bars of my ringneck parrot's cage. "Here you go, Polygon."

My bird waddles his perch shouting, "God save the Queen."

"Loyal and smart." I say as I wiggle the pear enticingly. "You need more roughage in your diet, my feathered friend. Can't have you getting backed up again."

"Mother, could you please stop talking to that blasted bird and finish our conversation?"

Polygon hops off his perch, wraps his claws around my arthritic knuckle, and begins to peck at the fruit. Touch is the sensation of touch I miss more than conversation. Which is strange, considering the complaints I lodged with Martin when I felt worn out by the constant pawing of third graders. Guess that goes to show how easy it is to take something for granted until it's gone.

I release the fruit and Polygon waddles toward his seed dish with a full mouth. "At least my bird listens."

Charlotte sighs. "I bought the riding mower to help you. The doctor said the strain of *pushing* a mower over that huge yard is putting your heart at risk." Her continued exasperation rattles me more than her exaggeration. "Obviously, power equipment isn't the answer."

"Anyone could've confused all those fancy pedals."

"You're seventy-two, Mother." She always manages to cite my age before overstepping the boundaries we've set in place. "There's no shame in admitting that you can no longer keep up with three hundred acres of rugged hill country."

I wipe the window with the sleeve of my robe and gaze at the pasture dotted with patches of this spring's fading bluebonnets. "No one was hurt."

"This time." The strain in her voice is as irritating as a mandatory fire drill.

"You want me to let the place grow up around my ears?"

"Of course not." She sighs to emphasize the stress I'm obviously adding to her very busy day. "But since you refuse to consider a move, I have to hire you some help."

I bite my tongue. Silence won't end this conversation with Charlotte, but it won't hurt her to believe it's the only defense I have left.

"I'm worried about you, Mother."

Charlotte's deep inhalation is my cue to take a seat because the recounting of my shortcomings that she feels honor bound to recite has grown into a rather long list. "In the last six months, you've flushed your dentures down the toilet."

"Just the lowers."

"You got lost on the way to town."

"Winnie found me and hauled me back home." I add, "Long before dark."

"I hate to think what would have happened if you hadn't run out of gas along her mail route."

Overstated dramatics always harden my resolve. Ask any child who was unlucky enough to have me as their teacher. "No law against trying a change of scenery."

"You don't like change, Mother," my daughter snips. "That's why we can't seem to have an honest and productive conversation about your future."

I sink into the chair and rest my elbow on the table. "Just because you think the old gray mare *ain't* what she used to be..." I cringe at that I've resorted to using slang. "...that doesn't mean I want to leave my home of forty-five years and move to Washington, D.C., Charlotte Ann."

Surely it wasn't that many years ago that Martin and I ignored a weathered *No Trespassing* sign, climbed an old, barbed-wire fence, shed our clothes, and jumped from a thirty-foot bluff with the abandon of two people with more nerve than sense. The moment our naked bodies slid into the crystal-clear water, we knew the Fossil Ridge Ranch was meant to be our little piece of heaven.

I've loved and lost on this land. I can't bear to leave any of it.

"I know this is hard," Charlotte whispers.

"How *could* you know? You only come home once a year."

"Mother, that's not true. I've flown to Texas four times since Thanksgiving. And if you don't start cooperating, I'm going to have to come home in April as well."

Without following the school calendar dates scramble in my head. "Four times?"

"Yes," she says. "I have a job, a teenager, and a marriage I'm trying to keep together. I can't keep dropping everything to..."

Her pause is my cue to say something that will soothe her conscience, to grant a pass that lets her off the hook. That's been our unspoken agreement for twenty-some years. I don't get a pass. She doesn't get a pass. That way neither one of us has to forgive the other. Slocums are like that. Charlotte may have taken on that fancy McCandless surname when she married a good-for-nothing playboy, but roots deep as ours are tougher than weeds to yank out.

Charlotte's quiet. But I can hear her ripping the tiny gold treble clef back and forth on the thin silver chain around her neck. She's gearing up to issue my ultimatum. I suppose I should take some consolation in the fact that she still wears the little trinket I gave her years ago. Perhaps we're not completely lost to each other.

"If you want to stay on the Fossil Ridge, then you'll have to give this new guy a chance."

"He's already mowed over the bluebonnets in my front yard. They're beautiful this year, but he cut them down before they could seed. Next thing you know, he'll be toppin' my myrtles."

"I'll text him to be more careful. Please, for my peace of mind, can you just give this new guy a try?" Charlotte's breathing is becoming more rapid. Any minute she'll blow, unable to leave well enough alone. "That's all I ask."

"That's all?" Anger pumps through my veins and I spring from the chair, a taut rubber band aimed at the class bully. "If you call stripping my independence *guarding my heart*, Charlotte Ann, I'll take my chances with high cholesterol and a push mower."

I hang up the phone with a decisive slam and march to the counter. Sticky juice oozes from what remains of the mutilated mound of fruit.

Whatever happened to family taking care of family? My neighbor LaVera's grown son takes care of her. Bo isn't pressuring his mother to leave her place, nor does he pawn off his responsibilities on hired help.

I swallow a bite of the vanilla-sweet flesh then poke a sliver through the bars of the birdcage. "Charlotte won't be satisfied until I sign over complete control of *my* life."

My bird abandons his preening and snatches his breakfast with his bright red beak.

"Sweet Moses," I snap. "Say something, Polygon!"

I know better than to encourage this feathered chatterbox to speak with his mouth full, but this traitorous deed by Charlotte has me in such a stew I'm willing to risk the undoing of my bird's etiquette training.

For once, Polygon behaves and remains silent. Although pleased the hours I've invested in my parrot's behavior has finally begun to pay off, I admit that at this very moment a word of encouragement, even a feathery nod would be a comfort. How many years has it been since I've had someone in my corner?

More than I care to count.

The screaming kettle gyrates above the gas flame. "We'll show Charlotte who can still take care of themselves, won't we, Polygon?"

I pour boiling water over a twice-used tea bag then wait for the water to brown. It's maddening that my life has come to recycling tea bags. Martin and I had planned to spend our golden years spoiling a passel of grandchildren. I shuffle to the fridge. My gnarled finger traces the photograph that curls beneath the World's Best Teacher magnet stuck to the door.

The little beauty sitting beside me and Charlotte is my only grandchild. Aria was eight when this photo was taken nearly five years ago. I haven't seen this little lioness in months. Busy teenager stuff, her mother claims. But I can't help but wonder if Ari has also outgrown her need for me. After all, she's probably taller than me by now, and well-past the age of appreciating anything I could teach her. And I'd planned to teach her so much. Her times tables. Piano scales. How to tell a barn swallow from a sparrow. The best way to free a fossil from the limestone that lines the river.

Some dreams are best forgotten.

I return to my tea, splurge and add a cube of sugar, then lift the rose-patterned porcelain cup to my lips.

My apple-green bird tilts his head, his beady eyes assessing my brewing storm. I blow steam in his direction. "You won't leave me, will you, Polygon?"

"C'mere." He waddles the length of his perch. "Pretty girl."

I rest the cup on a saucer and stick my finger through the wires and stroke the soft down above his beak. "If only family were as loyal."

I'd give anything to have my Martin pat my fanny as I wash up the supper dishes. Or have my ambitious Caroline hug my neck after I admire her work. Or have my sweet Charlotte crawl into my lap and beg for another song on the piano.

"Thank you for sticking it out, Polygon." Through tears, I look my bird in the eye. "Once I send Charlotte's new hire packing, we'll have our life back."

"Be nice." Polygon gives my finger a peck.

"Traitor." I recoil at his siding with Charlotte. "This has to be done, Polygon. And, no matter what anyone tries to tell me, I'm still the woman to do it."

About the Author

Lynne Gentry knew marrying a pastor might change her plans. She underestimated how much serving alongside him in fulltime ministry would change her life. An author of numerous novels, short stories, and dramatic works, Lynne travels the country as a professional acting coach and inspirational speaker. Because Lynne's imagination loves to run wild, she also writes historical fiction and contemporary medical thrillers.

Lynne lives in Dallas with her husband and medical therapy dog. She counts spending time with her two grown children and their families her greatest joy.

You're invited to join her adventures into these other worlds at **www.lynnegentry.com**.

Lynne loves visiting Book Clubs.

To invite her to join your book club discussion email her at lynne@lynnegentry.com.

Made in the USA
Monee, IL
26 September 2024